W0044050

Oxford Skills World

Reading with Writing 4

Katie Foufouti

OXFORD
UNIVERSITY PRESS

OXFORD
UNIVERSITY PRESS

198 Madison Avenue
New York, NY 10016 USA

Great Clarendon Street, Oxford, OX2 6DP, United Kingdom

Oxford University Press is a department of the University of Oxford.
It furthers the University's objective of excellence in research, scholarship,
and education by publishing worldwide. Oxford is a registered trade
mark of Oxford University Press in the UK and in certain other countries

ISBN: 978 0 19 411352 6 Student Book with Workbook

Printed in China

This book is printed on paper from certified and well-managed sources

ACKNOWLEDGMENTS

*Oxford University Press would like to thank all of the teachers whose opinions helped to
inform this series, and in particular, the following reviewers:* Soo Ah Chung, Hwarang
Elementary School; Marta Juanet, Betania-patmos; Sedef Toksöz Kaykın,
Denizli Pamukkale Unv Egitim Vakfi okullari (PEV Koleji); Jeehee Moon,
T.T.R.; Jacob Rod, WILS Language School; Yuechun Wang, Phonenix City
International School

Cover illustration and main character illustrations by: Shane McGowan/The
Organisation

Back cover photograph: Oxford University Press building/David Fisher

Student Book

Illustrations by: Scott Angle/Carole Newman & Associates pp.18, 36, 37, 39,
44, 78; David Arumi/Astound Us pp.38, 46, 55, 56, 57; Charlene Chua pp.27,
28, 29; Lalena Fisher pp.14, 23, 24, 54, 66, 67, 69, 70, 71, 74; Peter Francis/
MB Artists pp.41, 43, 88; Angie Jones pp.15, 25, 65; Anthony Lewis/MB Artists
pp.8 (ExA), 26, 42, 68; Margeaux Lucas/MB Artists pp.51, 52, 53, 58, 85; Juan
Moreno/MB Artists pp.8 (ExB), 9, 10, 11, 72; Susanna Rumiz/Lemonade
Illustration pp.30, 79, 80, 81

*The Publishers would like to thank the following for their kind permission to reproduce
photographs and other copyright material:* 123rf: 8 (ice hockey gear/Valeriy
Lebedev), (girl with helmet/Val Thoermer), 9 (playing badminton/Engkritchaya
Sirawatmetha), 13 (mitt/Steve Collender), (bat/klotz), 22 (firefighter hosing
flames/Akhararat Wathanasing), 23 (daisy and thermometer/Ying Feng
Johansson), (sky/Nataliia Kravchuk), (thermometer/Alexey Filatov), 27 (lake/
efired), (foggy forest/Matthew Gibson), 32 (bay/Anastasia Tsarskaya), 41 (lady
boarding coach/dolgachov), 50 (puppies/Waldemar Dabrowski), 51 (brown
curly hair/subbotina), (blonde wig/Aleksandr Belugin), (girl with bangs/
Alina Shilzhyavichyute), 69 (girl flying kite/Josef Muellek), 79 (petrol station/
Carolyn Franks), (man alighting subway train/Michael Rosebrock), 83 (Golden
Gate bridge/Luciano Mortula), (gift shop exterior/radub85); Alamy: cover
(father and daughter canoeing/Hero Image Inc), 13 (softball batter and team/
Jon Osumi), (softball batter/Jon Osumi), 34–35 (astronauts spacewalking/
Stocktrek Images, Inc.), 48 (toddlers crawling/Wavebreak Media ltd), 64 (soccer
team celebrating win/STOCK4B GmbH), 76–77 (gondolas in Venice/Scott
Wilson); Getty: 6–7 (children playing table tennis/KidStock), 9 (professional
soccer match/Image Source), 13 (boy catching ball/Shoji Fujita), (girls playing
basketball/kali9), 16 (team huddle/kali9), 20–21 (giant sequoia/jimveilleux),
41 (girl reading novel/Kaori Ando), 64 (girl with soccer ball/asisecit), 65 (man
at mixing desk/quavondo), 83 (Buddhist temple/chadchai rangubpai); Oxford
University Press: 9 (ice hockey game/Shutterstock), 27 (tropical beach/
Shutterstock), (rainbow/bogdan ionescu), 37 (erupting volcano/Ammit Jack),
40 (satellite/3Dsculptor), 41 (suitcase/Marquisphoto), (cityscape/turtix),
55 (older couple/Jamie Hooper), 79 (subway train/1986OmegaTribe), 83,
84 (Burj Khalifa/Sophie James); Shutterstock: 9 (children playing ice hockey/
Lucky Business), (basketball team/Monkey Business Images), (girl with
basketball/Dmytro Surkov), (girls playing soccer/Ron Hilton), 12 (boy playing
ice hockey/Click Images), 13 (girl doing yoga/Kotin), 19 (pencil, reused on
pp.47, 61, 75, 89/almaje), 22 (blue backpack/Andrew Buckin) 22 (family
walking/Monkey Business Images), 23 (woodland through the seasons/
Skylines), (Earth from space/Atakan Yildiz), (sun/Passakorn Umpornmaha),
27 (rainforest/badahos), (condensation on glass/Pompaem Gogh), 37 (rocks/
AlexeyNikitin1981), (rocket/Nostalgia for Infinity), (sailboat/Alvov), (racing
car/Kuznetsov Alexey), 41 (stamped passport/sfeichtner), (builders consulting
plans/Monkey Business Images), 50 (brothers laughing/Giulio_Fornasar),
51 (girl's ponytail/Lara Barrett), (shoulder length hair/Gelpi), (freckles/
Irina Bg), 55 (two girls comparing height/ZouZou), (girl with straight hair/
Chin Kit Sen), (man with moustache/Monkey Business Images), (man with
beard/iordani), (boy with glasses/Happy Together), 60 (father and son/
wavebreakmedia), 62–63 (group using smartphones/DisobeyArt), 69 (picking
up money/cunaplus), (shopping mall/MikeDotta), (eating popcorn at cinema/
Nestor Rizhniak), (man tenpin bowling/Romaset), (advert/Alex Gorka),
78 (family skiing/dotshock), 79 (ferry in port/CDL Creative Studio), 82 (New
York city ferry/All kind of people), (tourist visiting Statue of Liberty/Juergen
Faelchle), 83, 84 (woman at salon/KPG_Payless), 83, 84 (cable car/Peppinuzzo),
83, 84 (department store/Wayne0216), 86 (Sydney Opera House at night/
Tooykrub)

Workbook

Illustrations by: Scott Angle/Carole Newman & Associates pp.96, 100; David
Arumi/Astound pp.99, 101; Lalena Fisher pp.103, 107, 108 (Ex2b and Ex4a),
109; Angie Jones pp.108 (Ex1,2a,3 and 4b)

*The Publishers would like to thank the following for their kind permission to reproduce
photographs and other copyright material:* 123rf: 92 (playing badminton/
Engkritchaya Sirawatmetha), (girl with helmet/Val Thoermer), 94 (mitt/
Steve Collender), 96 (sky/Nataliia Kravchuk), (daisy and thermometer/Ying
Feng Johansson), (thermometer/Alexey Filatov), 100 (Flatiron building/Rafael
Ben-Ari), 102 (lady boarding coach/dolgachov), 104 (girl with bangs/Alina
Shilzhyavichyute), (blonde wig/Aleksandr Belugin), 104, 105 (brown curly hair/
subbotina), 112 (petrol station/Carolyn Franks), (Golden Gate bridge/Luciano
Mortula), (man alighting subway train/Michael Rosebrock), 113 (Istanbul at
sunset map/Ahmet Ihsan Ariturk), 114 (Flatiron building/Rafael Ben-Ari), (Golden
Gate bridge/Luciano Mortula), (gift shop exterior/radub85); Alamy: 92 (softball
batter/Jon Osumi), (soccer team celebrating win/STOCK4B GmbH), 94 (softball
batter/Jon Osumi), 105 (action figure/JG Photography), 111 (gondolas in
Venice/Scott Wilson); Getty: 92 (professional soccer match/Image Source),
94 (boy catching ball/Shoji Fujita), 100 (girl reading novel/Kaori Ando),
102 (girl reading novel/Kaori Ando); Oxford University Press: 92 (ice hockey
game/Shutterstock), 96 (satellite/3Dsculptor), 98 (rainbow/bogdan ionescu),
(tropical beach/Shutterstock), 102 (cityscape/turtix), (suitcase/Marquisphoto),
106 (older couple/Jamie Hooper), 112 (subway train/1986OmegaTribe);
Shutterstock: 83 (woman at salon/KPG_Payless), 91 (girls playing soccer/Ron
Hilton), 92 (girl with basketball/Dmytro Surkov), 92, 93 (basketball team/
Monkey Business Images), 94 (girl doing yoga/Kotin), 95 (rainforest/badahos),
96 (Earth from space/Atakan Yildiz), (sun/Passakorn Umpornmaha), (rocks/
AlexeyNikitin1981), 97 (axe and stump avatar/AF studio), 98 (condensation on
glass/Pompaem Gogh), (rainforest/badahos), 100 (rocket/Nostalgia for Infinity),
(rocks/AlexeyNikitin1981), (racing car/Kuznetsov Alexey), (sailboat/Alvov),
(eating popcorn at cinema/Nestor Rizhniak), 104 (girl's ponytail/Lara Barrett),
(girl with straight hair/Chin Kit Sen), (shoulder length hair/Gelpi), (freckles/
Irina Bg), 106 (man with moustache/Monkey Business Images), (two girls
comparing height/ZouZou), 110 (shopping mall/MikeDotta), (eating popcorn at
cinema/Nestor Rizhniak), (picking up money/cunaplus), (advert/Alex Gorka),
112 (ferry in port/CDL Creative Studio), (two girls comparing height/ZouZou),
114 (woman at salon/KPG_Payless)

Table of Contents

Hi! I'm Olly.

Hi, I'm Molly!

Introduction

Welcome to Oxford Skills World

Oxford Skills World: Reading with Writing is a flexible paired skills course that takes students on a journey toward independent learning, providing them with strategies and support to reach their goals.

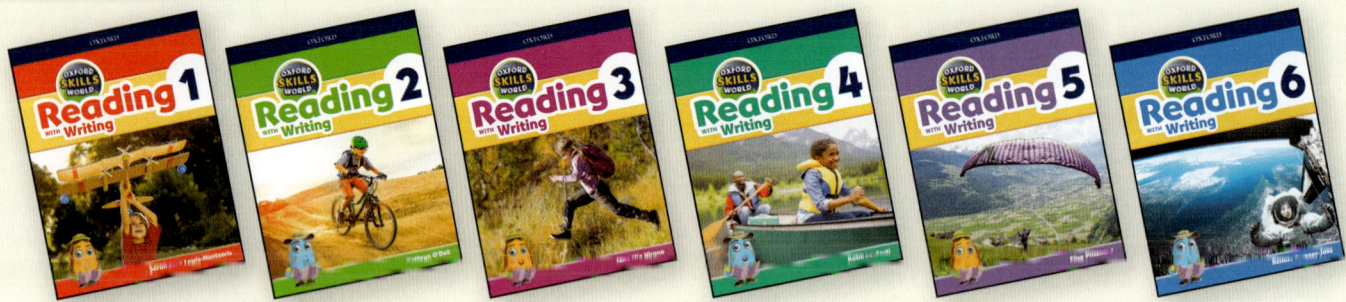

For Students

- Student Book / Workbook
- Student's website with downloadable audio and extra resources
  www.oup.com/elt/oxfordskillsworld

For Teachers

- Downloadable Teacher's Pack with instructional support, assessment, professional development videos, projects, and writing resources
- Classroom Presentation Tool
- Teacher's website with downloadable audio and extra resources
  www.oup.com/elt/teacher/oxfordskillsworld

Be the Leader on Your Skills Adventure!

Hi! We're Olly and Molly, your skills adventure guides. We help you reach your goals by introducing new reading and writing strategies, asking helpful questions, and giving friendly reminders. Most importantly, we cheer you on every step of the way! Let's go!

Quick Guide

Inside Each Topic

Topic Opener

Theme-based topics provide high-interest content relevant to students' lives.

My Goals introduces students to the objectives of each unit in the topic.*

Fun characters, Olly and Molly, encourage 21st century skills like critical thinking, collaboration, and communication.

Students answer questions to activate prior knowledge and think critically.

Get Ready to Read • Read

Reading Goals are strategies students can apply to any text.

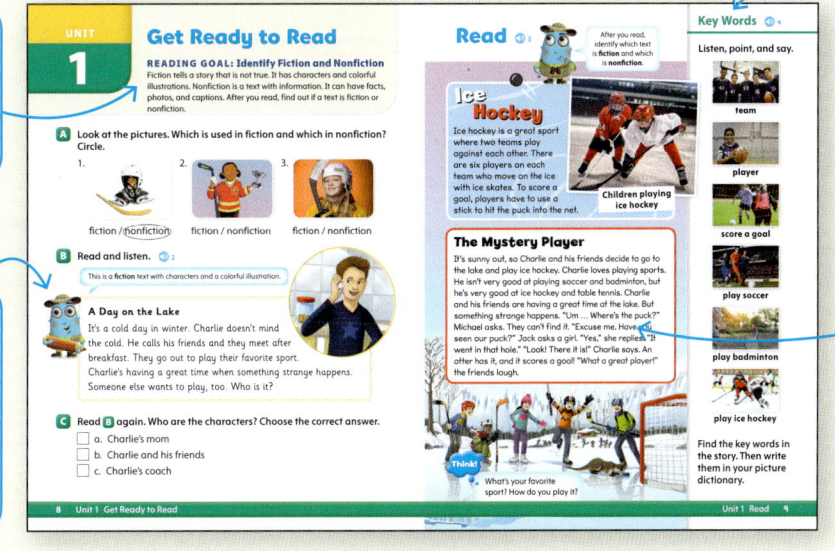

Olly and Molly guide students as they learn and apply new reading strategies.

Students learn new vocabulary for each text and complete the picture dictionary at the back of the book.

Students apply strategies to high-interest fiction and nonfiction texts, think critically about what they read, and make connections to their own lives.

*Each topic contains two thematically related units.

Quick Guide

Understand

Students increase their comprehension of the text by applying reading strategies to what they have read.

Students complete activities to strengthen their understanding of the unit's vocabulary.

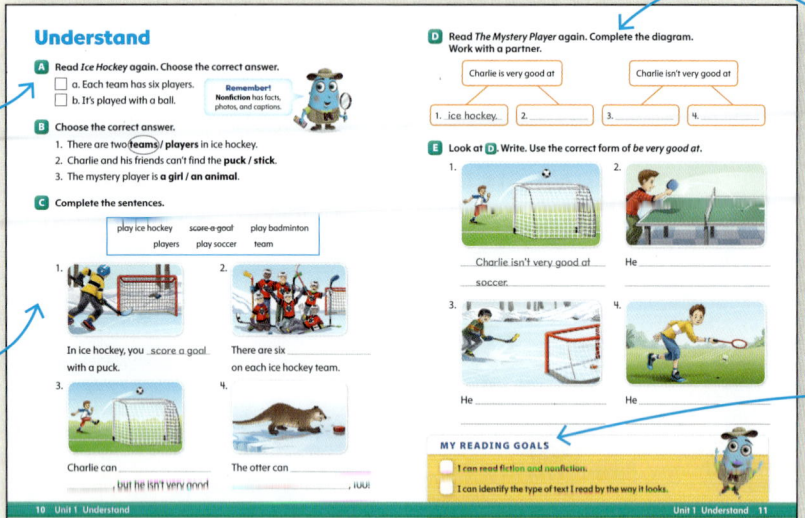

Students demonstrate comprehension of the unit's text, vocabulary, and grammar.

At the end of each unit, students assess the progress they have made toward achieving their goals.

Reading Check

With helpful reminders from Olly and Molly, students apply the **Reading Goals** from both units to a new text.

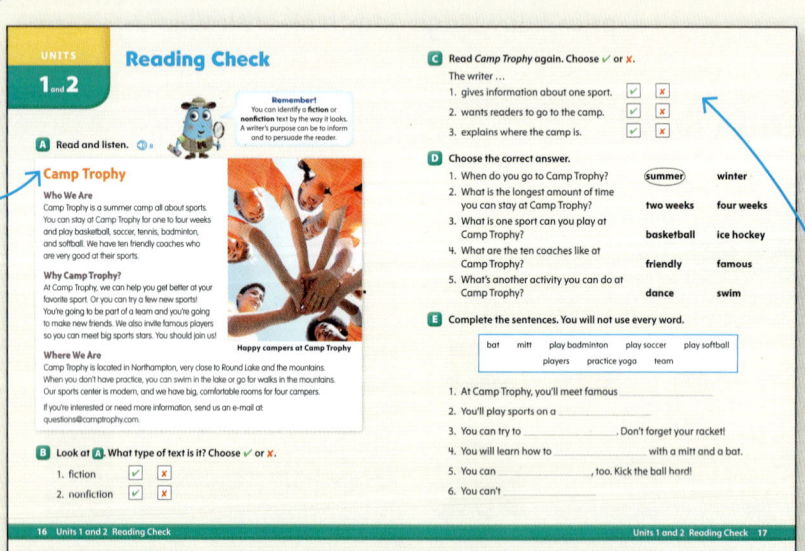

Students complete activities to boost comprehension and vocabulary application.

Get Ready to Write • Write

Writing Goals prepare students to write in different genres.

Writing Tips provide guidance on grammar, punctuation, and mechanics and help students write fluently and accurately.

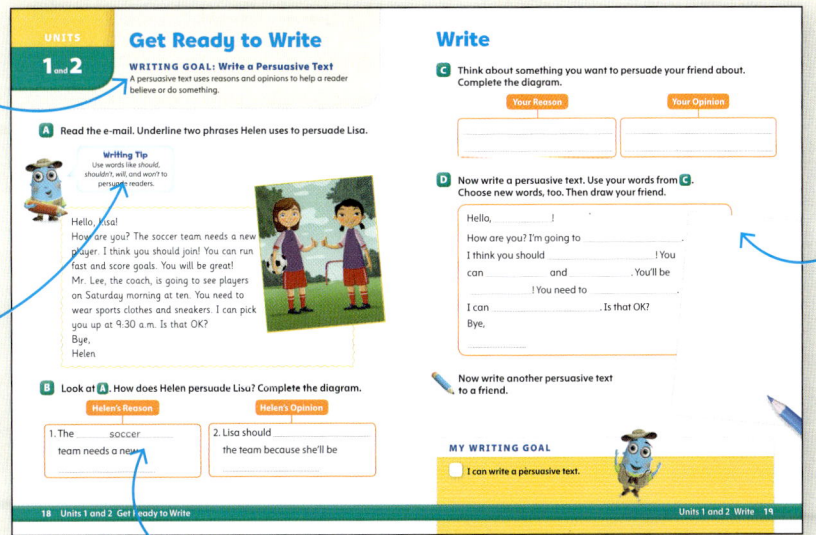

Scaffolded writing passages help students accomplish their writing goals.

Students use graphic organizers to comprehend model writing texts and to organize their thoughts for their own writing.

Workbook

Workbook pages at the end of the book provide more opportunities for students to apply their **Reading Goals** and boost comprehension.

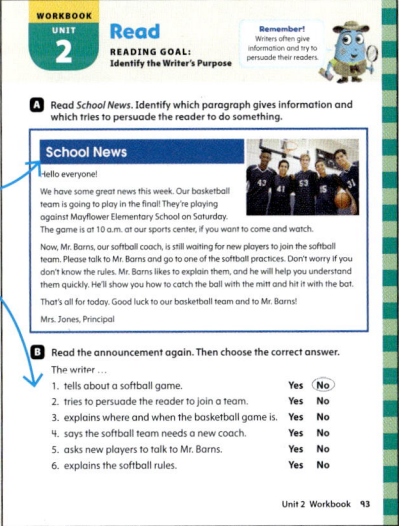

Additional activities provide extra opportunities for vocabulary comprehension and usage.

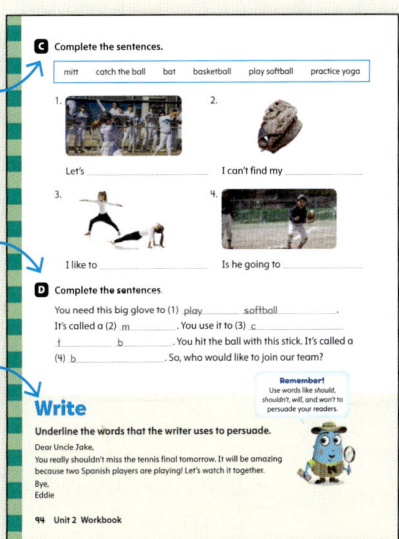

Students apply the topic's **Writing Tip** to ensure proper usage in their own writing.

Crazy About Sports!

MY GOALS

UNIT 1

- Read the text *Ice Hockey*
- Read the story *The Mystery Player*
- Identify fiction and nonfiction

UNIT 2

- Read the blog post *A Softball Star*
- Identify the writer's purpose

WRITE

- Write a persuasive text

A Look at the picture. What do you see?

1. What are the children doing?
2. How does the girl feel?

FUN FACT

Table tennis started in England in the 1880s. Today, people play it all around the world. The best players can hit the ball so it travels at 27 kilometers per hour!

B Read the Fun Fact. Then answer the questions.

1. Where did table tennis start?

2. What sports or games do you like to play inside?

Think, Pair, Share
What sports or type of exercise would you like to try?

Get Ready to Read

READING GOAL: Identify Fiction and Nonfiction
Fiction tells a story that is not true. It has characters and colorful illustrations. Nonfiction is a text with information. It can have facts, photos, and captions. After you read, find out if a text is fiction or nonfiction.

A Look at the pictures. Which is used in fiction and which in nonfiction? Circle.

1.

fiction / (nonfiction)

2.

fiction / nonfiction

3.

fiction / nonfiction

B Read and listen. 🔊 2

This is a **fiction** text with characters and a colorful illustration.

A Day on the Lake

It's a cold day in winter. Charlie doesn't mind the cold. He calls his friends and they meet after breakfast. They go out to play their favorite sport.
Charlie's having a great time when something strange happens. Someone else wants to play, too. Who is it?

C Read **B** again. Who are the characters? Choose the correct answer.

☐ a. Charlie's mom
☐ b. Charlie and his friends
☐ c. Charlie's coach

Read 🔊 3

After you read, identify which text is **fiction** and which is **nonfiction**.

Ice Hockey

Ice hockey is a great sport where two teams play against each other. There are six players on each team who move on the ice with ice skates. To score a goal, players have to use a stick to hit the puck into the net.

Children playing ice hockey

The Mystery Player

It's sunny out, so Charlie and his friends decide to go to the lake and play ice hockey. Charlie loves playing sports. He isn't very good at playing soccer and badminton, but he's very good at ice hockey and table tennis. Charlie and his friends are having a great time at the lake. But something strange happens. "Um … Where's the puck?" Michael asks. They can't find it. "Excuse me. Have you seen our puck?" Jack asks a girl. "Yes," she replies. "It went in that hole." "Look! There it is!" Charlie says. An otter has it, and it scores a goal! "What a great player!" the friends laugh.

Think!

What's your favorite sport? How do you play it?

Listen, point, and say.

team

player

score a goal

play soccer

play badminton

play ice hockey

Find the key words in the story. Then write them in your picture dictionary.

Understand

A Read *Ice Hockey* again. Choose the correct answer.

☐ a. Each team has six players.

☐ b. It's played with a ball.

Remember!
Nonfiction has facts, photos, and captions.

B Choose the correct answer.

1. There are two **teams** / **players** in ice hockey.

2. Charlie and his friends can't find the **puck / stick**.

3. The mystery player is **a girl / an animal**.

C Complete the sentences.

play ice hockey	~~score a goal~~	play badminton
players	play soccer	team

1.

In ice hockey, you _score a goal_
with a puck.

2.

There are six _____
on each ice hockey team.

3.

Charlie can _____
_____, but he isn't very good.

4.

The otter can _____
_____, too!

D Read *The Mystery Player* again. Complete the diagram. Work with a partner.

Charlie is very good at	Charlie isn't very good at

1. ice hockey. 2. _____ 3. _____ 4. _____

E Look at **D**. Write. Use the correct form of *be very good at*.

1.

Charlie isn't very good at soccer.

2.

He _____

3.

He _____

4.

He _____

MY READING GOALS

- [ ] I can read fiction and nonfiction.
- [ ] I can identify the type of text I read by the way it looks.

Get Ready to Read

READING GOAL: Identify the Writer's Purpose

Every writer has a purpose. One purpose is to inform, or give information. Another purpose is to persuade, or make you believe or do something. When you read, ask, *Why did the writer write this?*

A **Read the note. Why did Nick write it? Choose the correct answer.**

☐ a. to tell his mom about practice

☐ b. to get his mom to bring lunch

Hi, Mom!
I have ice hockey practice at 11:30 a.m., so don't wait for me to have lunch. We're going to practice every day this week. Bye!
Nick

B **Read and listen.** 5

Writers often want to persuade their readers.

Hi, Sam,
I hope you're free Saturday because I have an important game. You have to come and see me play, OK? I won't play well if you're not there. After the game, we'll go out for ice cream! Why don't you bring your brother, too?
Nick

C **Read B again. What is Nick trying to persuade Sam to do? Choose ✔ or ✗.**

1. eat ice cream

2. go to the game

3. bring his brother

Read  🔊 6

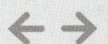

What does Emma tell you about? What does she want you to believe?

www.softballstar.osw/emma

A Softball Star by Emma Reed

My name's Emma, and I'm on my school's softball team. People often ask me, "Why do you like to play softball?" and "Do you play every day?" Here are my answers.

Well, softball is interesting and fun! You have to be fast and careful. You need to be good at catching the ball with the mitt and hitting it with the bat. I also like it because you play it with other players. You should try it!

We have softball practice on Mondays, Wednesdays, and Fridays after school. On Saturdays we usually have an important game. I don't play softball every day, but I exercise every day. On Tuesday afternoons, I like to play badminton with my brother. On Thursdays, I like to play basketball at school. On Sundays, I like to practice yoga with my mom and watch sports on TV — but only if all my homework is done!

Think!

Do you prefer to play sports with others or by yourself? Why?

Key Words 🔊 7

Listen, point, and say.

play softball

catch the ball

mitt

bat

basketball

practice yoga

Find the key words in the blog post. Then write them in your picture dictionary.

Understand

Remember!
While you're reading a text, think about the writer's **purpose**.

A Read *A Softball Star* again. Is Emma giving information? Choose **Yes** or **No**.

1. I'm on my school's softball team. (Yes) No
2. You should try it! Yes No
3. You need to be good at catching the ball. Yes No

B Choose the correct answer.

1. Why does Emma like softball?
   ☐ a. It's a slow sport. ☑ b. It's a team sport.
2. How often does Emma have softball practice?
   ☐ a. three times a week ☐ b. four times a week
3. How does Emma relax on Sunday?
   ☐ a. She watches sports on TV. ☐ b. She does yoga with friends.

C Complete the sentences with key words. Then match.

1. These girls __play softball__ on a team.

2. This is a _____. You use it to catch the ball.

3. They're playing _____ in the gym.

4. This is a _____. You use it to hit the ball.

a.

_____

b.

____1____

c.

_____

d.
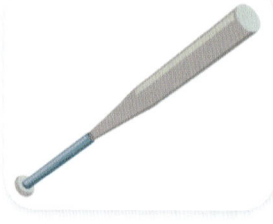
_____

D Read *A Softball Star* again. Complete the table. Work with a partner.

Emma likes to ...	During the week	On the weekend
1. play basketball	✔	
2. watch TV		
3. practice yoga		
4. play badminton		

E Look at **D**. Write. Use *likes to*.

1.

On the weekend, Emma

_____

2.

She _____ ,
too.

3.

During the week, she

_____

4.

She _____ ,
too.

MY READING GOALS

☐ I can read the blog post.

☐ I can identify the writer's purpose.

Reading Check

Remember!
You can identify a **fiction** or **nonfiction** text by the way it looks. A writer's purpose can be to inform and to persuade the reader.

A **Read and listen.** 🔊 8

Camp Trophy

Who We Are

Camp Trophy is a summer camp all about sports. You can stay at Camp Trophy for one to four weeks and play basketball, soccer, tennis, badminton, and softball. We have ten friendly coaches who are very good at their sports.

Why Camp Trophy?

At Camp Trophy, we can help you get better at your favorite sport. Or you can try a few new sports! You're going to be part of a team and you're going to make new friends. We also invite famous players so you can meet big sports stars. You should join us!

Happy campers at Camp Trophy

Where We Are

Camp Trophy is located in Northampton, very close to Round Lake and the mountains. When you don't have practice, you can swim in the lake or go for walks in the mountains. Our sports center is modern, and we have big, comfortable rooms for four campers.

If you're interested or need more information, send us an e-mail at: questions@camptrophy.com.

B Look at **A**. What type of text is it? Choose ✔ or ✘.

1. fiction   ✔   ✘

2. nonfiction   ✔   ✘

C Read *Camp Trophy* again. Choose ✔ or ✗.

The writer …

1. gives information about one sport. ☑ ✔ ☐ ✗

2. wants readers to go to the camp. ☑ ✔ ☐ ✗

3. explains where the camp is. ☑ ✔ ☐ ✗

D Choose the correct answer.

1. When do you go to Camp Trophy? (summer) winter

2. What is the longest amount of time you can stay at Camp Trophy? two weeks four weeks

3. What is one sport can you play at Camp Trophy? basketball ice hockey

4. What are the ten coaches like at Camp Trophy? friendly famous

5. What's another activity you can do at Camp Trophy? dance swim

E Complete the sentences. You will not use every word.

bat	mitt	play badminton	play soccer	play softball
	players	practice yoga	team	

1. At Camp Trophy, you'll meet famous _____

2. You'll play sports on a _____

3. You can try to _____. Don't forget your racket!

4. You will learn how to _____ with a mitt and a bat.

5. You can _____, too. Kick the ball hard!

6. You can't _____

Get Ready to Write

WRITING GOAL: Write a Persuasive Text
A persuasive text uses reasons and opinions to help a reader believe or do something.

A Read the e-mail. Underline two phrases Helen uses to persuade Lisa.

Writing Tip
Use words like *should*, *shouldn't*, *will*, and *won't* to persuade readers.

Hello, Lisa!
How are you? The soccer team needs a new player. I think you should join! You can run fast and score goals. You will be great!
Mr. Lee, the coach, is going to see players on Saturday morning at ten. You need to wear sports clothes and sneakers. I can pick you up at 9:30 a.m. Is that OK?
Bye,
Helen

B Look at **A**. How does Helen persuade Lisa? Complete the diagram.

Helen's Reason

1. The _____ soccer _____ team needs a new
_____

Helen's Opinion

2. Lisa should _____
the team because she'll be
_____

Write

C Think about something you want to persuade your friend about. Complete the diagram.

Your Reason	Your Opinion

D Now write a persuasive text. Use your words from **C**. Choose new words, too. Then draw your friend.

Hello, _____ !

How are you? I'm going to _____ .

I think you should _____ ! You

can _____ and _____ . You'll be

_____ ! You need to _____ .

I can _____ . Is that OK?

Bye,

_____

✏️ Now write another persuasive text to a friend.

MY WRITING GOAL

☐ I can write a persuasive text.

The Living Earth

MY GOALS

UNIT 3

- Read the text *Colorful Forests*
- Find the main ideas and details

UNIT 4

- Read the story *Finding My Way*
- Make predictions

WRITE

- Write a descriptive text

 A **Look at the picture. What do you see?**

1. How tall do you think the trees are?
2. Would you like to see trees this big? Why or why not?

FUN FACT

The biggest trees in the world grow in California, USA. They're called sequoia trees, and some are thousands of years old! A big sequoia can be almost 100 meters tall and 11 meters around.

B **Read the Fun Fact. Then answer the questions.**

1. How long do sequoia trees live?
2. Are there big trees like these where you live?

Think, Pair, Share
What's your favorite type of plant? Why?

Get Ready to Read

READING GOAL: Find the Main Ideas and Details
Each paragraph in a text has a main idea and details.
Details explain the main idea of a paragraph. When you read,
find the details to understand the main idea.

A Look at the picture.
Choose the main idea.

☐ a. The weather in forests changes
a lot.

☐ b. Forest fires are a big problem
today.

☐ c. A lot of wild animals live in forests.

B Read and listen. 🔊 9

This is the **main idea** of the text. The **details** explain it.

Important Forests

Forests are important for all living creatures.
They're home to plants, tall trees, and all
types of animals, from big bears to small squirrels. They give us
wood and clean air. And they're fun to visit, too! You can go for
walks, have picnics, and sometimes even go camping!

C Read **B** again. What detail explains the main idea?
Choose the correct answer.

☐ a. You can have a picnic in the forest.

☐ b. Forests are fun to visit.

☐ c. Forests give us clean air.

Read

What's the **main idea** of each paragraph? Underline it.

Colorful Forests

Forests are some of the most beautiful places on Earth. I'm in a forest now, on a warm day in summer. The sun is high in the sky. There are beautiful, tall trees with shiny, green leaves. I can smell the flowers and the grass. I can hear the birds singing and the bugs buzzing.

This forest is going to be very different in a few months. In fall, the trees change color to orange, yellow, and red. As the weather gets cooler, the leaves start falling to the ground. Most people like forests in fall because the leaves are colorful. But I think fall is worse than spring or summer. And winter is better than spring and summer!

Forests are very pretty in snowy weather. They turn white and everything's quiet. Some animals, like bears and bats, go to sleep, or hibernate. When spring arrives, the animals wake up, and trees grow new leaves again.

Think!

Where is the closest forest in your area? What animals live there?

Key Words

Listen, point, and say.

Earth

warm

the sun

sky

weather

cool

Find the key words in the text. Then write them in your picture dictionary.

Understand

A Read *Colorful Forests* again. Look at the first paragraph. Choose one of its details.

☐ a. The Earth is a beautiful place.

☐ b. The trees are pretty in the summer.

> **Remember!**
> **Details** explain the **main idea** of the paragraph.

B Choose the correct answer.

1. In a forest, it's **quiet / noisy** in spring.

2. Trees lose their leaves in **cold / hot** weather.

3. In winter, forests turn **white / brown**.

C Complete the sentences.

| cools | the sun | sky | Earth | weather | warm |

1.
Forests are beautiful places

on _____

2.
It can feel hot when

_____ is out.

3.
The weather _____

down in fall.

4.
The _____ in winter is

good for skiing.

D Read *Colorful Forests* again. Complete the diagram.

The best / worst season

1. The writer thinks that fall is _____ spring and summer.

2. The writer thinks that winter is _____ spring and summer.

E Look at **D**. Write. Use *better than* or *worse than*.

1.

I think ___winter is better___ ___than spring.___ (winter / spring)

2.

I think _____ _____ (fall / summer)

3.

I think _____ _____ (summer / winter)

4.

I think _____ _____ (spring / fall)

MY READING GOALS

☐ I can read the text.   ☐ I can identify the main idea and its details in each paragraph.

Get Ready to Read

READING GOAL: Make Predictions

A prediction is what you think will happen. When you read, use clues to make predictions about how the story will continue and how it will end. Clues can be a story's title, words, and pictures.

A Look at the pictures. Order the story.

B Read and listen. How is the story going to end? 12

The story's picture is a clue that helps you **predict** the ending.

We Found It!

"Oh, no!" said Harry as he opened the front door to his house. His mom was reading a book when he came in. "What's wrong?" she asked. He explained that he forgot his umbrella in the park. "Don't worry. We'll find it." When the rain stopped, they went to look for it. It was still by the tree, where he left it.

C Read **B** again. What other clues helped you make predictions? Choose ✔ or ✗.

1. The title, *We Found It!*

2. Harry opened the front door.

3. Harry's mom said they would find it.

Read  🔊 13

What clues can you find to help you **predict** the ending? Underline them.

Finding My Way

"As a young student," Maya's dad began, "I spent three weeks in Brazil in the tropical rain forest."

"What was it like?" Maya asked.

"Well, it was really humid and hot, but I didn't mind," he answered. "I slept in a tent and I studied bugs and plants. One afternoon, I went for a walk alone and saw the most beautiful bird! I followed it for a while until it suddenly disappeared. *Oops!* I thought. I was lost and it was getting dark. I tried to sleep under a tree next to a lake, but I couldn't. It was rainy and the animals made loud noises all night."

"So, what happened?" Maya asked.

"Well, the next day I was really tired and hungry," he said. "It was foggy in the morning. When it cleared, I saw a bright rainbow and the same beautiful bird! It flew above my head and I decided to follow it again. I felt that it wanted to help me find my way. A little while later, I found my tent again."

Think!

Have you ever gotten lost? What happened?

Listen, point, and say.

tropical

rain forest

humid

lake

foggy

rainbow

Find the key words in the story. Then write them in your picture dictionary.

Understand

Remember!
The story's title, pictures, and words can help you **predict** the ending.

A Read *Finding My Way* again. Do these clues help you predict the ending? Choose **Yes** or **No**.

1. It was really humid and hot.   **Yes   No**

2. I tried to sleep under a tree.   **Yes   No**

3. It wanted to help me find my way.   **Yes   No**

B Choose the correct answer.

1. Who got lost in the rain forest?

☐ a. Maya   ☐ b. Maya's dad

2. What was Maya's dad following?

☐ a. a bird   ☐ b. an insect

3. Why couldn't Maya's dad sleep?

☐ a. It wasn't quiet.   ☐ b. It was hot.

C Complete the sentences with key words. Then match.

1. Maya's dad lived in a _____ _____ when he was young.

2. Maya's dad tried to sleep under a tree next to a _____, but he couldn't.

3. He couldn't see in the morning because it was _____

4. He took a photo of the _____ in the sky.

a.

_____

b.

_____

c.

_____

d.

_____

D Read *Finding My Way* again. Complete the diagram.
Work with a partner.

1. Maya's dad couldn't sleep because	→	the animals ___made___ loud noises.

2. When the fog cleared,	→	he _____ a rainbow.

E Look at **D**. Write. Use the correct form of the verb.

1.

The animals _____ loud noises. (make)

2.

Maya's dad _____ sleep. (can't)

3.

The fog _____ in the morning. (clear)

4.

Maya's dad _____ a rainbow. (see)

MY READING GOALS

☐ I can read the story.　　☐ I can predict the story's ending by looking at the title, words, and pictures.

Reading Check

Remember!
Find the **main idea** and **details** to understand a story better. Use the title, pictures, and words to **predict** the ending.

A Read and listen. 15

The Caring Wolf

Poppy was a little girl who loved forests. She loved to pick flowers when it was warm and the sun was high in the sky. She also liked to run through the trees when it was rainy.

Yesterday, it was snowy and foggy. Poppy was helping her dad make a cake. "Take some cake to Grandma," he said. "But be careful." On the way, Poppy stopped at the frozen lake. Her grandma's house was on the other side. "Hmm … It's faster if I walk on the lake," Poppy thought.

Crack! The ice broke. "Help!" Poppy yelled. Nobody could hear her — except for a scary wolf. "Go away!" she shouted, but the wolf came closer and closer. He had a branch in his mouth. He wanted to help Poppy! She grabbed the branch. The wolf started to pull the little girl out of the frozen water.

B What's the main idea of the first paragraph? Choose ✔ or ✘.

1. Why Poppy likes forests.

2. Where Poppy lives.

3. How Poppy met a wolf.

C Look at the clues. How will the story end? Choose ✔ or ✘.

1. The wolf will eat Poppy. ✔ ✘

2. The wolf will swim in the lake. ✔ ✘

3. The wolf will save Poppy. ✔ ✘

D Choose the correct answer.

1. What's the weather like in the forest in winter?
   ☐ a. cold ☐ b. humid

2. Poppy walked on the frozen lake because she wanted to
   ☐ a. arrive more quickly. ☐ b. go ice skating.

3. What was Poppy scared of?
   ☐ a. the cold water ☐ b. the wolf

4. How did the wolf help Poppy?
   ☐ a. with his tail ☐ b. with a branch

E Unscramble and match.

1. g f g y o   • a. not cold
   ___foggy___

2. s n u   • b. It's blue and sometimes there
   _____   are clouds.

3. y s k   • c. big pool of water, usually near
   _____   trees

4. r w m a   • d. what it's like when the fog
   _____   rolls in

5. k a e l   • e. It's in the sky during the day.
   _____

Get Ready to Write

WRITING GOAL: Write a Descriptive Text

A descriptive text can be about a place. To help readers imagine a place, describe what they can see, hear, smell, and feel in that place.

A **Read the text. Underline the adjectives.**

> **Writing Tip**
> Use adjectives to describe something. Adjectives are words like *pretty*, *loud*, and *happy*.

A Beautiful Place

by Yusuf

My favorite place is Kabak Bay. It's a beautiful beach in Turkey. There aren't big hotels around, so it's really quiet. It has soft sand and clear, blue water. You can see small fish swimming in the sea. There's a forest around the bay and the trees smell great! From the beach, you can go for a walk to some amazing waterfalls. There are six pools where you can swim. It's fantastic!

B **Look at A. What does Yusuf describe? Complete the diagram.**

1. ___beautiful___ beach

2. _____ blue water

3. trees smell _____

4. no hotels, so it's _____

5. _____ waterfalls

6. _____ sand

see, hear, smell, and feel

Write

C Think about your own favorite place. What can you see, hear, smell, and feel there? Complete the diagram.

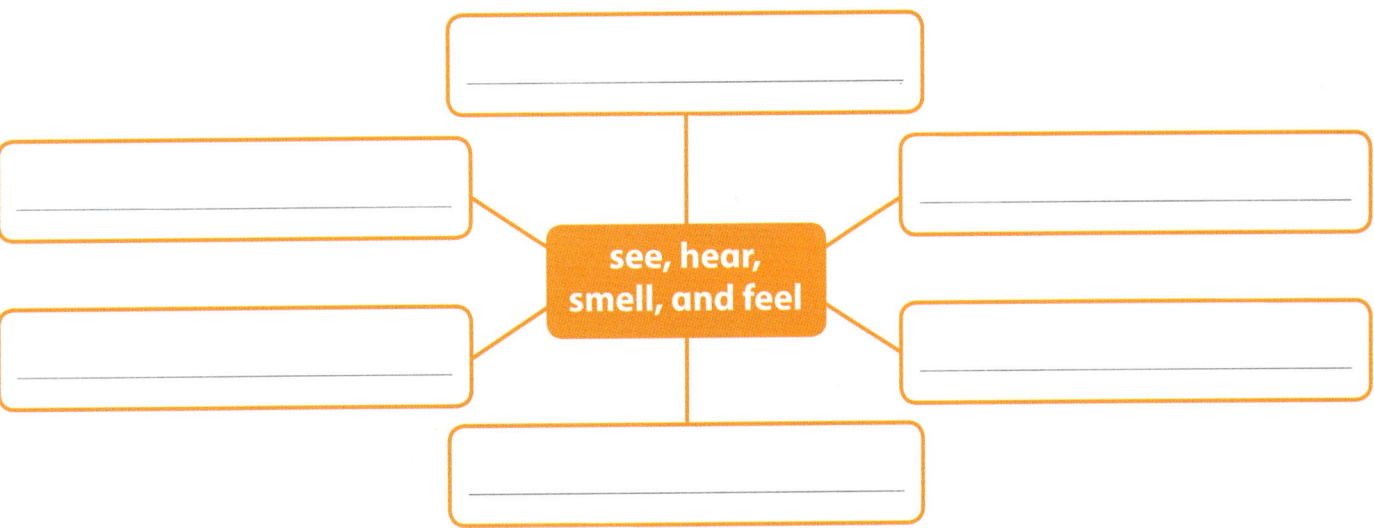

see, hear, smell, and feel

D Now write about your favorite place. Use your ideas from **C**. Choose some new adjectives, too. Then draw a picture of your place.

My favorite place is _____.

It's a _____ in _____.

There are(n't) _____. It's really

_____. It has _____ and

_____. You can _____.

There's _____. It's fantastic!

Now write a descriptive text about a place you don't like.

MY WRITING GOAL

☐ I can write a descriptive text about a place.

Let's Go to Space!

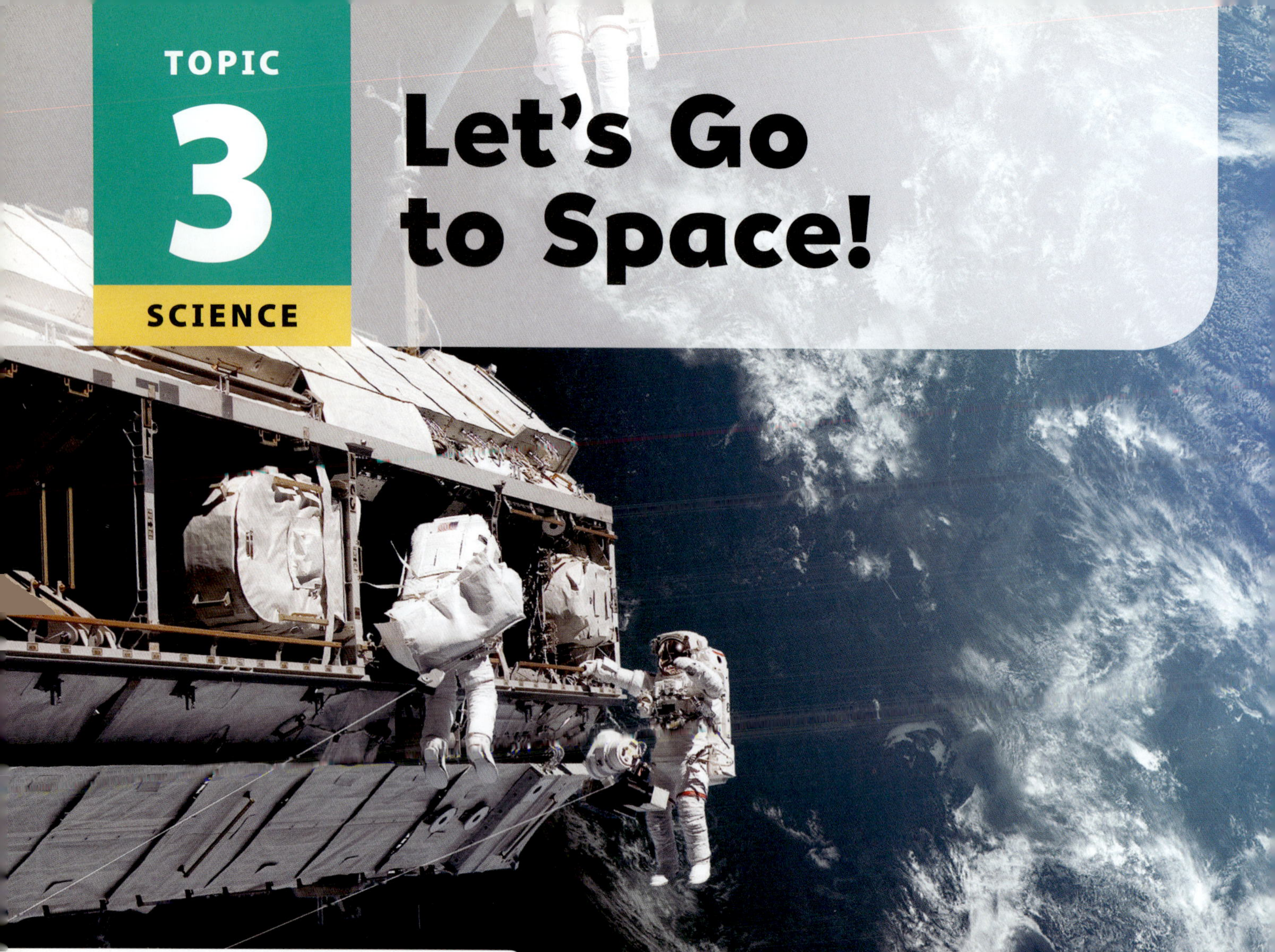

MY GOALS

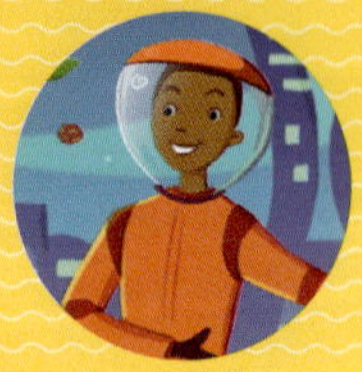

UNIT 5
- Read the story *Planet Zork*
- Find similes

UNIT 6
- Read the text *What the Future Holds*
- Guess unknown words

WRITE
- Write an opinion text

A Look at the picture. What do you see?

1. Where are the astronauts?

2. What are the astronauts doing?

FUN FACT

Astronauts live on the Space Station when they get to space.

It takes 90 minutes for the Space Station to go around Earth. That means astronauts see the sun set and rise 17 times a day!

B Read the Fun Fact. Then answer the questions.

1. What is the Space Station?

2. How long does it take to go around Earth?

3. Would you like to be an astronaut?

Think, Pair, Share
How many planets can you name?

Get Ready to Read

READING GOAL: Find Similes

A simile uses *like* or *as* to compare two different things. For example, *The rocket is as big as a whale* is a simile. When you read, look for similes. They will help you imagine the story.

A Look at the pictures. Choose the best simile for each picture.

1.

a. He felt as light as a balloon.

b. He felt as heavy as a rock.

2.

a. The food was as soft as toothpaste.

b. The food smelled like flowers.

3.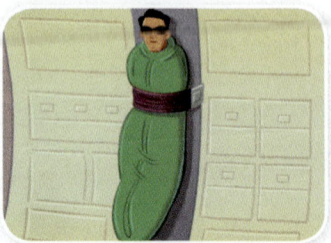

a. He worked like a dog.

b. He slept like a baby.

B Read and listen. 🔊 16

This is a **simile**. It uses *like* to compare two different things.

A Journey in Space

Mario looked out of the window at Earth.
It looked like a ball you could hold in one hand.
For a minute, he thought about his family, so far
away. But then he got back to work — he still had a lot to do!

C Read **B** again. What two things does the simile compare and why? Choose the correct answer.

☐ a. Earth and a ball because Earth is full of air

☐ b. Earth and a ball because Earth looks small

☐ c. Earth and a ball because Earth bounces

Read 🔊 17

Find two **similes** in the story. Underline them.

Planet Zork

"This is it!" said Naoko. She climbed out of the spacecraft and then helped her son, Hiro. "This planet isn't that different from Earth," he said and took a photo of some rocks.

"Welcome!" said a friendly man. "Are you ... Deran?" asked Naoko. "That's right. I'm your guide for today. Jump in!" Deran said.

"Wow! Cool car!" said Hiro. It went fast like a rocket. Naoko and Hiro looked around the city. They saw strange buildings and people sailing boats in the sky. "What's that? Can we climb it?" asked Hiro. "Oh, that's our pink volcano! It's hard to climb. It's as soft as a pillow. But we can try!" Deran said.

"Do you want to be an astronaut when you're older?" Deran asked Hiro. "No, I want to drive a race car on Earth," Hiro answered. "Space is fun, but it's too strange for me," and they all laughed.

Think!

- Would you like to spend a day with Deran on Planet Zork? Why or why not?

Key Words 🔊 18

Listen, point, and say.

spacecraft

rocks

rocket

sail a boat

volcano

drive a race car

Find the key words in the story. Then write them in your picture dictionary.

Understand

A Read *Planet Zork* again. Which simile is about Deran's car? Choose the correct answer.

☐ a. as soft as a pillow

☐ b. fast like a rocket

> **Remember!**
> Look for *like* and *as* to find the **similes**.

B Choose the correct answer.

1. Hiro thinks Earth and Planet Zork are **different / similar**.

2. Deran is Naoko and Hiro's **guide / waiter**.

3. Hiro wants to **be an astronaut / drive a race car** someday.

C Complete the sentences.

| volcano | rocks | drive a race car | sail a boat | rocket | spacecraft |

1.

Deran's car is fast like a

_____

2.

Deran likes to visit the

_____

3.

Naoko and Hiro arrived on

Planet Zork in a _____

4.

Hiro took a photo of some

_____

D Read *Planet Zork* again. Work with a partner. Complete the diagram.

1. When Hiro's older, → he wants to

_____

_____

2. When Hiro's older, → he doesn't want to

_____

_____

E Look at **D**. Write. Use *wants to* or *doesn't want to* and the verb.

1.

Hiro _____

the pink volcano. (climb)

2.

Hiro _____

an astronaut. (become)

3.

Hiro _____

sailing. (go)

4.

Hiro _____

a slow car. (drive)

MY READING GOALS

☐ I can read the story.

☐ I can identify similes by looking for *like* and *as*.

Get Ready to Read

READING GOAL: Guess Unknown Words
When you read, you might find words you don't know. If this happens, look at the words before and after them. These words can help you guess the meanings of the words you don't know.

A Read the sentences. What are meteorites? Choose the best meaning.

> Every year thousands of meteorites travel through space and hit Earth. They make large holes on our planet because they are so big and fast. Scientists say that some of these big rocks come from the moon or the planet Mars.

☐ a. Meteorites are planets.

☐ b. Meteorites are rocks.

☐ c. Meteorites are holes.

B Read and listen. 🔊 19

These words help you guess the meaning of *satellites*.

Will We Need Satellites in the Future?

Satellites are very useful. These big machines move around Earth in space. When you call a friend, your voice goes to a satellite in space, then back to Earth, and then to your friend's phone. I think we will still use satellites 100 years from now.

C Read **B** again. What other words help you understand the meaning of *satellites*? Choose ✔ or ✘.

1. are very useful

2. move around Earth in space

3. 100 years from now

Read  20

Which words help you understand the word *passport*?

www. in100yrs.osw/spacetravel

What the Future Holds

Today's question: What will life be like in 100 years? Post your answer here!

Hi! I think 100 years from now we will travel around the galaxy in rocket buses. They will take passengers into space to visit different planets, like Mars. We will still need to show a passport with our photo to travel around space, like we do now when we visit other countries. Also, we will have suitcases that fly, so we won't have to carry them. It'll be a great way to travel!

Miray

Well, I'm reading a novel about people destroying Earth and building cities in space. I think this might happen in 100 years. There won't be any trees or animals on Earth and we won't have air to breathe. So people will build houses in space, maybe on the moon. We will see Earth, but we won't be able to visit it.

Eric

Think!

What do *you* think life will be like in 100 years?

Key Words 21

Listen, point, and say.

travel around

passenger

suitcase

read a novel

city

build a house

Find the key words in the blog. Then write them in your picture dictionary.

Understand

Remember!
If you don't know a word, look at the words before and after it to help you understand it.

A Read *What the Future Holds* again. Think about the words. Choose Yes or No.

1. A *passport* is a card that allows you to drive.   **Yes**   **No**
2. To *destroy* means to break something apart.   **Yes**   **No**
3. If you *breathe*, air moves in and out of your body.   **Yes**   **No**

B Choose the correct answer.

1. How does Miray think people will travel to space?
   ☐ a. by bus   ☐ b. in spacecraft

2. Where did Eric get his idea from?
   ☐ a. a movie   ☐ b. a book

3. Where does Eric think we will live in the future?
   ☐ a. on the moon   ☐ b. on Earth

C Complete the sentences with key words. Then match.

1. Miray thinks we will _____ the galaxy.

2. She thinks we will have flying _____

3. Eric thinks we will _____ on the moon.

4. He _____ about people living in space.

a.
_____

b.
_____

c.
_____

d.
_____

D Read *What the Future Holds* again. What do Miray and Eric predict? Complete the diagram with *will* or *won't*.

1. We _____won't_____ carry suitcases.

2. We _____ travel around the galaxy.

Future Predictions

3. We _____ live on the moon.

4. We _____ visit Earth.

E Look at **D**. Write. Use *will* or *won't*.

1.

We _____

2.

We _____

3.

We _____

4.

We _____

MY READING GOALS

☐ I can read the blog.

☐ I can guess the meanings of unknown words by looking at words before and after.

Reading Check

Remember!
You can find **similes** by looking for *like* or *as*. **Guess the meaning** of an unknown word by looking at the words before and after it.

A Read and listen. 🔊 22

Alex's Dream

It was late, but Alex couldn't put the book down. He was reading a novel: *Journey into an Unknown Galaxy.* A meteorite was going to hit a big city on Planet XYZ6b! The meteorite was a rock traveling through space. It was only a few thousand kilometers away when … zzzzz … Alex fell asleep.

"Where am I?" he asked in his dream. He was driving a race car. "Ha-ha! I didn't know I could drive!" he laughed. He saw a big volcano far away in front of him. Snow covered it like a white blanket. Alex wanted to get closer so he could see it better. "I'll just drive the car and get closer!" When he finally stopped, he got out to look around. "Ouch!" Alex hit his toe on something hard. A sign was on the ground. It said *Welcome to Planet XYZ6b.*

B Look at the text. Are these similes? Choose ✔ or ✘.

1. traveling through space

2. like a white blanket

3. driving a race car

C What words help you understand *meteorite*? Choose ✔ or ✗.

1. a rock traveling through space　　　✔　✗

2. He was reading a novel.　　　✔　✗

3. It was only a few thousand kilometers away.　✔　✗

D Choose the correct answer.

1. What was Alex doing before he fell asleep?　　　　　**watching TV**　**reading**

2. What was the meteorite going to hit?　**Earth**　**Planet XYZ6b**

3. What was the meteorite?　**a rock**　**a planet**

4. How did Alex feel about driving a race car?　　**surprised**　**worried**

5. What did Alex do to get closer to the volcano?　**he walked**　**he drove**

6. Where did Alex travel to in his dream?　**Planet XYZ6b**　**Earth**

E Complete the sentences.

volcano	drive a race car	galaxy	city
passenger	reading a novel	rock	spacecraft

1. Alex fell asleep when he was _____

2. The title of the book is *Journey into an Unknown* _____

3. A big _____ was going to hit Planet XYZ6b.

4. The meteorite was going to hit a big _____ on Planet XYZ6b.

5. Alex decided to _____ to the mountain top.

6. Alex wanted to get closer to the _____

Get Ready to Write

WRITING GOAL: Write an Opinion Text

An opinion text tells how you feel about something. It includes an introduction sentence with your opinion, sentences with your reasons for that opinion, and a conclusion sentence.

A **Read the text.**

Writing Tip
Use transitions, such as *first*, *next*, and *in conclusion*, to organize your writing.

What Will Life Be Like in 100 Years?

I think life in 100 years will be great! First, I think we won't all live on Earth. We will live in big spacecraft and travel around the galaxy. We will come back to Earth to see friends and family. Next, we will have robots. We won't have to do housework or go shopping. The robots will do everything, and they will drive us to school and work. In conclusion, life will be easier in the future.

B **Look at A. Complete the diagram.**

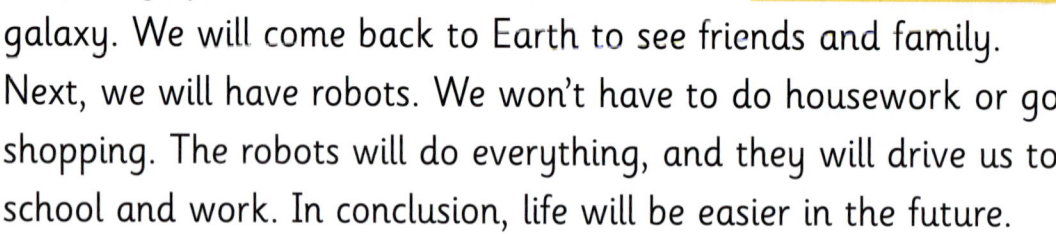

Reason:

2. First, _____

_____

Opinion:

1. Life in 100 years will be

 great.

Conclusion:

4. In conclusion, _____

_____

Reason:

3. Next, _____

_____

Write

C What do you think life will be like in 100 years? Complete the diagram.

Opinion:

Life in 100 years will be

_____

Reason:

First, _____

_____

Reason:

Next, _____

_____

Conclusion:

In conclusion, _____

_____

D Now write your own opinion text. Use your ideas from **C**.
Then draw a picture of the future.

I think life in 100 years will be _____

First, I think we _____

We _____

Next, _____

We _____

In conclusion, _____

Now write another opinion text about how we
will travel in space in the future.

MY WRITING GOAL

☐ I can write an opinion text.

Looks and Feelings

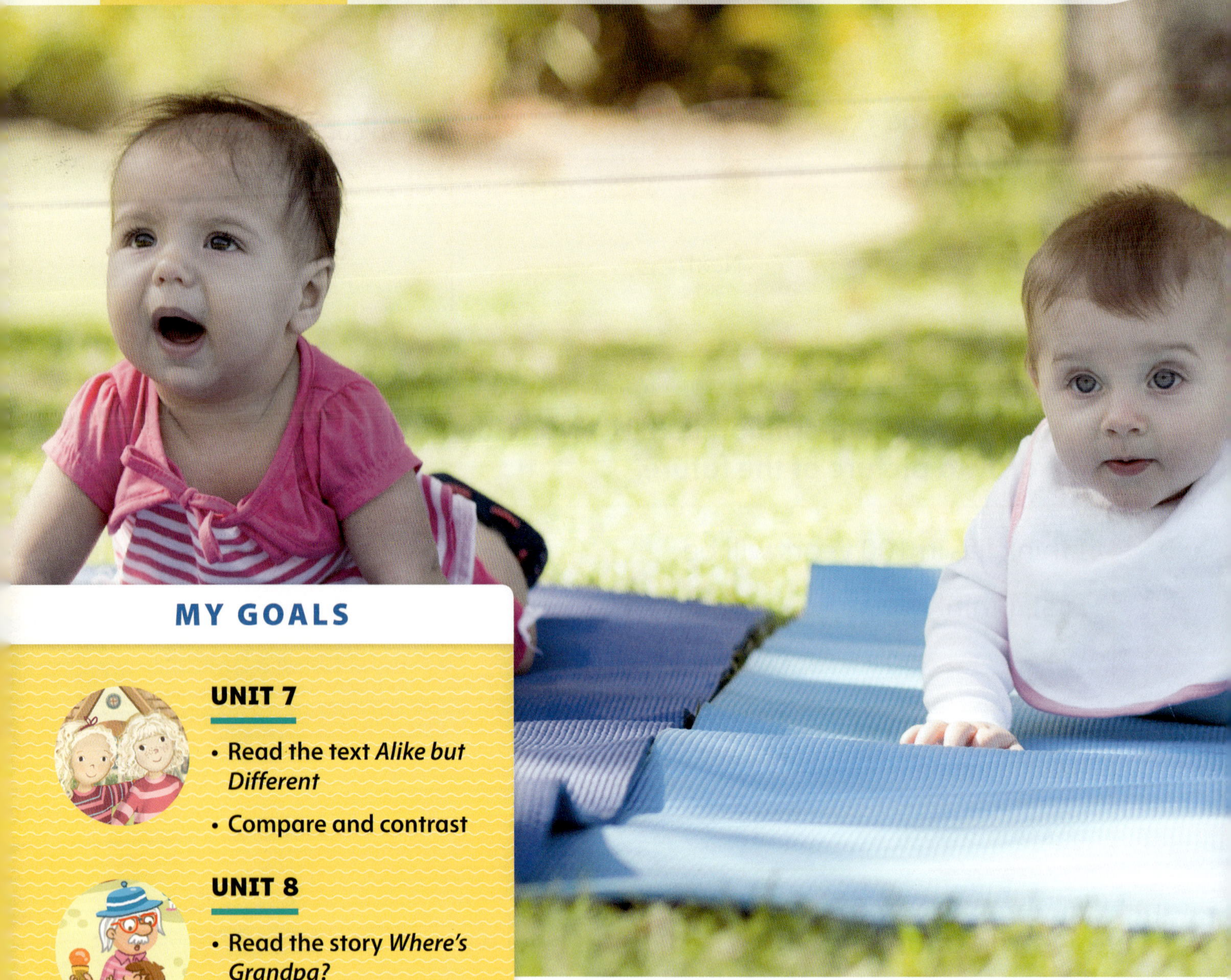

MY GOALS

UNIT 7

- Read the text *Alike but Different*
- Compare and contrast

UNIT 8

- Read the story *Where's Grandpa?*
- Understand characters

WRITE

- Write a descriptive text

A Look at the picture. What do you see?

1. Where are the babies?
2. How are they feeling?

FUN FACT

You have 206 bones in your body, but new babies have 300! As babies grow, their bones get harder and some stick together. Many babies are born with blue eyes, but they often change color after six months.

B **Read the Fun Fact. Then answer the questions.**

1. How many bones do babies have?

2. Are your eyes the same color as when you were born?

Think, Pair, Share
Where and when were you born?

Get Ready to Read

READING GOAL: Compare and Contrast

To *compare*, look at how things are the same. To *contrast*, look at how things are different. When you read, look for words like *both*, *too*, and *similar* to compare. Look for words like *but*, *different*, and *unlike* to contrast.

A **Look at the picture. Choose the correct sentence.**

☐ a. Milly and Dilly are both black.

☐ b. Milly is a puppy, but Dilly is a big dog.

☐ c. Milly has big ears and Dilly does, too.

B **Read and listen.** 🔊 23

Here are two similarities.

My Little Brother

My name is Michael, and Tim is my little brother. He's five years old. We share a bedroom and we like playing together. But he likes to play soccer and I don't. People say we look alike. We both have big brown eyes, but Tim has brown hair. My hair is blond! I have a small nose, and Tim does, too.

C **Read B again. How are Michael and Tim different? Choose the correct answer.**

☐ a. They have different hair colors.

☐ b. Their noses are different sizes.

☐ c. Their eyes are different colors.

Read 🔊 24

What similarities and differences can you find? Underline them.

Alike but Different

My best friends are Sophie and Katie. They're really fun and friendly, but there's one thing they don't like to hear: "You look so alike!" or "You're just like two peas in a pod!" It's true that they're twins, but they're not exactly the same.

They both have curly blond hair, but Katie's is longer and she always wears it in a ponytail. Sophie has shoulder-length hair and bangs. When I first met them, I had to look at their hair to know who was who.

I quickly saw more differences. Sophie has freckles, unlike Katie, who doesn't. Katie's eyes are brown and so are Sophie's, but Katie's are a little smaller. She's also a little shorter than Sophie. It's easy to tell who's who when you get to know them better. Katie and Sophie may be twins, but they really are very different.

Think!

What's your hair like? Who has hair like you in your family?

Listen, point, and say.

curly

blond

a ponytail

shoulder-length hair

bangs

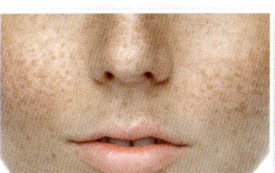

freckles

Find the key words in the story. Then write them in your picture dictionary.

Understand

A Read *Alike but Different* again. How are Sophie and Katie similar? Choose the correct answer.

Remember!
Both, *too*, and *similar* show similarities. *But*, *different*, and *unlike* show differences.

☐ a. They have curly blond hair.

☐ b. They have ponytails and bangs.

B Choose the correct answer.

1. Sophie and Katie are **sisters / friends**.

2. They have **similar / different** hairstyles.

3. The writer thinks they **are / aren't** the same.

C Complete the sentences.

| bangs | blond | a ponytail | curly | freckles | shoulder-length |

1.

Sophie has _____ on her face.

2.

Sophie's hair is _____

3.

Katie and Sophie both have _____ blond hair.

4.

Katie wears her hair in _____

D Read *Alike but Different* again. Complete the diagram.

1. _____Sophie_____ has
   ☑ shoulder-length hair
   ☑ freckles

2. They both have
   ☐ brown eyes
   ☐ curly hair

3. _____ has
   ☐ a ponytail
   ☐ smaller eyes

E Look at **D**. Write. Use *has* or *have*.

1.

Katie _____

2.

Sophie _____

3.

They _____

4.

They _____

MY READING GOALS

☐ I can read the text.   ☐ I can compare and contrast
                                 information by looking for
                                 both, *too*, *but*, and *unlike*.

Get Ready to Read

READING GOAL: Understand Characters
Characters have feelings, just like you do. When you read, ask yourself, *How does the character feel and why? Why does the character say this and act like this?* These questions will help you understand the story.

A Look at the pictures. How does the girl feel? Circle the correct word.

She's **sad / afraid**.   She's **bored / excited**.   She's **happy / angry**.

B Read and listen. 🔊 26

What Carlos says helps show his feelings.

A Scary Ride

"I don't know," said Carlos as he looked up at the roller coaster. "That's a really scary ride…"
"I think we should go on it," his aunt said. Carlos wasn't sure. He didn't like to climb tall trees or look down from tall buildings. "OK," he decided, and he loved it. "That was the best ride ever! Let's go on it again!"

C Read **B** again. How does Carlos feel? Choose ✔ or ✘.

1. at first happy and then worried   ✔ ✘
2. at first sad and then angry   ✔ ✘
3. at first scared and then excited   ✔ ✘

Read 27

What words and phrases help you understand Farook's feelings? Underline them.

Where's Grandpa?

"Yippee! I love going to the amusement park!" said Farook. "There are so many rides!" "And people, too!" said his dad. "If we lose each other, let's meet here, at the gate." "OK," replied Farook. "But … where's Grandpa?"

"Grandpa!" they shouted, but they couldn't find him. They stopped a clown. "Please help us! My grandfather's lost," Farook explained. "OK. What does he look like?" the clown asked. "Well, he's old and tall, and he has straight, white hair and a moustache. He doesn't have a beard," Farook said. "Is he wearing a hat?" she asked. "Yes. He usually wears his brown hat and a white shirt, but today he's wearing …" The clown smiled and said, "… a blue hat and a pink shirt. And he has red glasses." "That's right!" Farook said, surprised. "He's over there, buying ice cream!" she said.

"Grandpa! Where were you?" Farook cried. "Behind you. Why? What happened?" Grandpa asked, and they all laughed.

Think!

What should you do if you get lost?

Key Words 28

Listen, point, and say.

old

tall

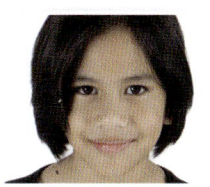

straight

a moustache

a beard

glasses

Find the key words in the story. Then write them in your picture dictionary.

Understand

A Read *Where's Grandpa?* again. Choose **Yes** or **No**.

1. "Yippee!" means that Farook is excited. **Yes**   **No**

2. They shout "Grandpa!" because they're worried. **Yes**   **No**

3. At the end, they laugh because they're sad. **Yes**   **No**

B Choose the correct answer.

1. Farook is excited because there are lots of
   ☐ a. people.   ☐ b. rides.

2. Farook's grandpa is wearing
   ☐ a. a blue hat.   ☐ b. a brown hat.

3. Farook's grandpa wasn't
   ☐ a. buying ice cream.   ☐ b. lost.

C Complete the sentences with key words. Then match.

1. Farook's grandpa has _____, white hair.

2. He's 75. He's _____

3. He has a _____, but not a _____

4. He has red _____. They help him read.

a.  _____

b.  _____

c.  _____

d.  _____

D Read *Where's Grandpa?* again. Complete the table.

Grandpa's clothes	
1. usually wears	a ___brown___ hat a _____ shirt
2. today is wearing	a _____ hat a _____ shirt

E Look at **D**. Write. Use *usually wears* or *is wearing*.

1.

Today, Farook's grandpa _____

_____ (shirt)

2.

He _____ _____

_____ (shirt)

3.

He _____

_____ (hat)

4.

Today, he _____

_____ (hat)

MY READING GOALS

☐ I can read the story. ☐ I can guess the characters' feelings by how they act and what they say in the story.

Reading Check

Remember!
Compare and contrast information in a text by looking for words like *both*, *too*, *but*, and *unlike*. Try to **understand the characters'** feelings by noticing how they act and what they say.

A Read and listen. 🔊 29

Now and Then

Mrs. Park looked at the tall, young woman in the photo. "Ah …" she said. The woman was about 22 years old, and she had a big, bright smile. Her hair was black and straight, and she kept it in a beautiful, long ponytail. She wore small glasses and pretty earrings. A tear ran down Mrs. Park's cheek. *I'm so silly,* she thought, and got up to make lunch.

Mrs. Park stopped at the mirror in the hallway. There, looking back at her, was the woman in the photo. Of course, she wasn't young anymore. She looked a lot older and her hair was different: shoulder-length and white as snow. But it was still straight. Her eyes seemed smaller, too, behind thicker glasses. "Look at that," said Mrs. Park. "I'm wearing the same earrings!" She smiled and saw that her smile was as big and bright as in that old photo.

B Look at the story. What is different about Mrs. Park now? Choose ✔ or ✘.

1. She has short hair.

2. She's not wearing glasses.

3. Her hair is white.

C Look at the first paragraph. How does Mrs. Park feel? Choose ✔ or ✗.

1. sad ✔ ✗   2. bored ✔ ✗   3. happy ✔ ✗

D Choose the correct answer.

1. Who's the woman in the photo?
   ☐ a. Mrs. Park   ☐ b. a friend of Mrs. Park

2. Mrs. Park is feeling sad because she is
   ☐ a. young.   ☐ b. old.

3. Mrs. Park's hair is like snow because it's
   ☐ a. white.   ☐ b. cold.

4. What makes Mrs. Park smile?
   ☐ a. her earrings   ☐ b. her glasses

5. What's still the same about Mrs. Park?
   ☐ a. her hair   ☐ b. her smile

E Unscramble and match.

1. l t a l _____   •   •   a. the opposite of *curly*

2. a h g t i s t r _____   •   •   b. the opposite of *young*

3. t y a l i n p o _____   •   •   c. people wear them to see better

4. e s s l a s g _____   •   •   d. a person who isn't short

5. d l o _____   •   •   e. hair that's down to your shoulders

6. s l o u h r d e - g n t e l h _____   •   •   f. hair that's tied up and hangs down

Get Ready to Write

WRITING GOAL: Write a Descriptive Text

A descriptive text can be about a person. It tells what the person looks like, what the person likes and dislikes, and what the person does.

A Read the description of a man. Underline what he likes. Circle what he doesn't like.

> **Writing Tip**
> Use *very* and *really* before adjectives to make them stronger.

My Uncle

This is my Uncle Walid. He has brown hair and a beard and moustache. His hair is short and straight and he doesn't wear glasses. He's 35 years old, so he's not very old. In this photo, he's wearing a T-shirt, but he usually wears a sweater. My uncle is a doctor. He works in a hospital, and in his free time, he really likes to play sports. He's very good at table tennis and basketball, but he doesn't like ice hockey. Sometimes we play basketball together.

B Look at **A**. Describe Uncle Walid. Complete the diagram.

1. Looks like: brown hair, moustache and beard

3. Likes: _____ _____

Uncle Walid

2. Job: _____ _____

4. Dislikes: _____ _____

Write

C Think about someone in your family. Complete the diagram.

Looks like: _____
_____

Likes: _____
_____

My _____

Job: _____
_____

Dislikes: _____
_____

D Now write your description. Use your ideas from **C**.
Then draw a picture of this person.

This is my _____.

_____ has _____
_____.

My _____ is a(n) _____.

_____ works _____.

_____ likes _____
_____.

_____ doesn't like _____
_____.

Now write a description of your best friend.

MY WRITING GOAL

☐ I can write a description of a person.

What Happened?

MY GOALS

UNIT 9

- Read an e-mail
- Understand cause and effect

UNIT 10

- Read the story *Three $20 Bills*
- Find the theme

WRITE

- Write a news article

A Look at the picture. What do you see?

1. What are the people doing with their phones?
2. Who are they sending messages to?

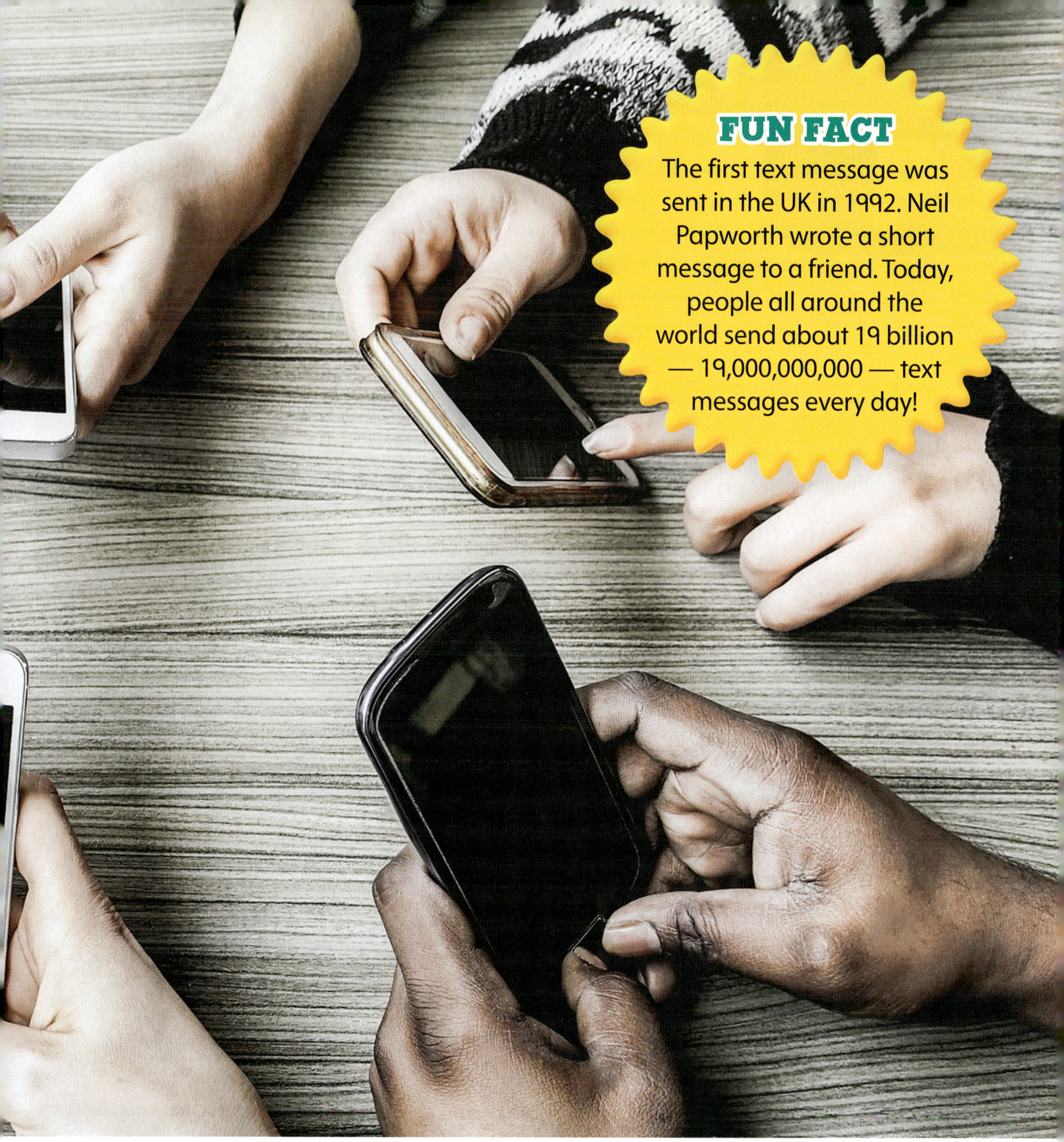

FUN FACT

The first text message was sent in the UK in 1992. Neil Papworth wrote a short message to a friend. Today, people all around the world send about 19 billion — 19,000,000,000 — text messages every day!

B **Read the Fun Fact. Then answer the questions.**

1. When did Neil Papworth send the first text?
2. Who do you send texts to and what about?

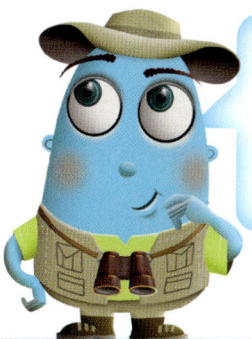

Think, Pair, Share

Do you have a cell phone? What do you use it for?

Get Ready to Read

READING GOAL: Understand Cause and Effect
A cause is why something happens. An effect is what happens because of the cause. When you read, look for words like *because*, *so*, and *if* to help you find causes and effects.

A **Look at the picture.**
Choose the correct sentence.

☐ a. The white team is happy because the green team scored a goal.

☐ b. The green team is upset because the white team scored a goal.

B **Read and listen.** 🔊 30

These are **causes** and (effects).

Know How to Lose

Hi, Jack,
We lost yesterday, so I'm really disappointed.
I knew it was going to be hard when Helen
stopped playing. She left the game because she hurt
her knee. I think she's doing OK. We lost 1–0. Coach Sanders
told me, "If you score a goal, we might win," but I didn't.
See you later,
Mary

C **Read B again. Why did Helen stop playing? Choose the correct answer.**

☐ a. She didn't want to play.

☐ b. She didn't score any goals.

☐ c. She hurt her knee.

Read 31

What are the **effects** and their **causes**? Underline them.

To: Nida
From: Samantha
Subject: A Good Excuse

Hi Nida,

I'm so sorry I didn't come to your house this morning to study. I slept late because last night we had a party at our house for my brother's birthday. Ed turned 18, so it was a big party. We even met a rock star — Ricky Berry! This is how it all happened.

Ed wanted a really cool party, so he asked DJ Sky to play music. He was very excited because DJ Sky is really famous. He's also a very good friend of Ricky Berry. Anyway, while DJ Sky was at the party, Ricky Berry sent him a text saying *Hi! Where are you? I'd like to see you about work.* DJ Sky gave him our address, and Ricky Berry came by our house. He signed his name on pieces of paper, and I took a picture of him! If you don't believe me, I'll show it to you at school.

See you tomorrow,

Samantha

Think!

Do you often say *sorry* to friends and family? What about?

Key Words 🔊 32

Listen, point, and say.

sleep late

have a party

meet a rock star

play music

send a text

take a picture

Find the key words in the story. Then write them in your picture dictionary.

Understand

A Read Samantha's e-mail again. Why didn't she go to Nida's house? Choose.

> **Remember!**
> Words like *because*, *so*, and *if* will help you find **causes** and **effects**.

☐ a. because she slept late

☐ b. because she went to a party

B Choose the correct answer.

1. Samantha was at her **sister's / brother's** party.

2. DJ Sky was **Ricky Berry's / Ed's** friend.

3. Samantha **was / wasn't** surprised to see Ricky Berry.

C Complete the sentences.

had a party	met a rock star	played music	sent a text
	took a picture	slept late	

1.

Samantha _____ of a rock star.

2.

The guests at Ed's party

_____

3.

Ed _____

4.

DJ Sky _____

D Read the e-mail again. Work with a partner. Complete the table.

Cause

1. Ricky Berry wanted to see DJ Sky _____so_____

Effect

he sent him a message.

Cause

2. _____ Nida doesn't believe Samantha,

Effect

Samantha will show her a picture.

Effect

3. Ed was excited _____

Cause

a famous DJ played music at his party.

E Look at **D**. Write. Use *because*, *so*, and *if*.

1.

Ricky Berry wanted to see DJ Sky _____.

2.

_____,

Samantha will show her a picture.

3.

Ed turned 18 _____

_____

4.

Ed was excited _____

_____

MY READING GOALS

☐ I can read the e-mail.   ☐ I can identify causes and their effects by looking for *because*, *so*, and *if*.

Get Ready to Read

READING GOAL: Find the Theme

The theme is a lesson you learn from a story. When you read, think about what a character does right or wrong. Then ask yourself, *What can I learn from this?*

A Look at the pictures. Order the story.

B Read and listen. 🔊 33

This is the **theme** of the story.

Melissa's Weekend

Melissa is sending her cousin a text. "I'll be at your house in five minutes," she writes. Watch out, Melissa! She almost has an accident. "Be careful, little girl!" the man on the bicycle shouts. "Watch where you're going." "Phew!" Melissa says and puts her phone in her pocket.

C Read **B** again. What did Melissa do wrong? Choose ✔ or ✘.

1. She went to her cousin's house.   ✔   ✘

2. She sent too many texts.   ✔   ✘

3. She was texting and didn't watch where she was going.   ✔   ✘

Read 34

What's the **theme** of the story? Underline it.

Three $20 Bills

"Look, Ali!" Dylan shouted. There were three $20 bills on the ground. It was the first time he found so much money. "Whose money is this?" Ali wondered. "I don't know, but it's ours now. Let's go shopping," Dylan answered.

The two friends went to the mall. First, they saw a movie and then they went bowling. Then they saw an advertisement for free ice cream, so they got some. After that they went to the beach and flew a kite.

The next day, in class …

"OK, everybody!" the teacher said. "Do you have the $60 for our school trip?" Zoe started crying. "I can't go, Miss Smith, because I lost the money in the schoolyard yesterday," she explained. "Oh no!" Dylan said. "How much?" Ali asked. "Sixty dollars," Zoe replied. The boys explained everything and said they were sorry. They gave Zoe's money back the next day, and she was able to go on the trip. The boys learned they shouldn't spend money they find.

Think!

What should you do when you find money?

Listen, point, and say.

find money

go to the mall

see a movie

go bowling

advertisement

fly a kite

Find the key words in the story. Then write them in your picture dictionary.

Understand

Remember!
What you learn from a character's actions will help you understand the **theme** of the story.

A Read *Three $20 Bills* again. Choose **Yes** or **No**.

1. Zoe was able to go on the school trip.   **Yes**   **No**

2. It was good that Ali and Dylan spent the $60.   **Yes**   **No**

3. It was good that Ali and Dylan gave the $60 back.   **Yes**   **No**

B Choose the correct answer.

1. Ali and Dylan found the money
   ☐ a. in class.   ☐ b. outside class.

2. The boys spent the $60 at the
   ☐ a. mall.   ☐ b. beach.

3. The $60 the boys found belonged to
   ☐ a. the teacher.   ☐ b. a student.

C Complete the sentences with key phrases. Then match.

1. The boys _____. Ali won!

2. They _____. It was very funny.

3. They _____ to spend the money.

4. They _____ at the beach.

a.
_____

b.
_____

c.
_____

d.
_____

 **Read *Three $20 Bills* again. What happened? Complete the diagram.**

1. First, Dylan

2. Then, Dylan and Ali

3. Next, they

4. After that, they

found some money.

_____
_____

saw a movie and
_____

_____
at the beach.

 Look at D. Write.

1.

Dylan and Ali _____
after visiting the mall.

2.

They _____
after reading an advertisement.

3.

They _____
and looked in a bunch of stores.

4.

Dylan _____
on the playground.

MY READING GOALS

☐ I can read the story.

☐ I can find the theme of a story by looking at what a character does.

Reading Check

Remember!
Identify **causes** and **effects** in a text by looking for words like *because, so,* and *if*. Ask yourself, *What can I learn from this story?* to find its **theme.**

A **Read and listen.** 🔊 36

A New Start

It was a beautiful, sunny day. Everyone was outside playing, except Diana. She was sitting at her desk, sending a text: *Mom, I don't like it here. I want to come home.* It was Diana's first day at Rosemary School, so she didn't have any friends.

Then two girls walked in — Lizzy and Jill. Jill had a party on Saturday and she was talking about it. "Some friends came to my house. We had food and listened to music. Then we went to the mall and we went bowling. It was great!" *How boring,* Diana thought. "Did you see a movie?" Lizzy asked. "No, we didn't, because we didn't have money," Jill explained. *Who cares?* Diana thought.

Lizzy looked at Diana. "You're new, right? What's your name?" Lizzy asked. "Um … yes. Diana," she said. "Come sit with us!" Jill said, and smiled. Diana didn't see her mom's text because she was chatting happily with her new friends.

B **Look at the story. What makes Diana feel unhappy? Choose ✔ or ✗.**

1. It's a sunny day.

2. She has no friends.

3. She's a new student.

C What lesson did Diana learn? Choose ✔ or ✘.

1. Go outside when it's warm.   ☑✔   ☐✘

2. Be friendly to people.   ☑✔   ☐✘

3. Don't have big parties.   ☑✔   ☐✘

D Choose the correct answer.

1. Who does Diana send a text to? **a friend** **her mom**

2. What did everyone do at Jill's party? **had food** **danced**

3. Why didn't Jill and her friends see a movie? **It was late.** **It was expensive.**

4. How does Diana feel when the girls are talking? **interested** **bored**

5. Why is Diana happy at the end of the story? **She has new friends.** **She got a text.**

E Complete the sentences.

found money	had a party	play music	see a movie
sent a text	take a picture	went bowling	went to the mall

1. Diana _____ saying she hated her new school.

2. Jill _____ and invited some friends.

3. After the party, they _____ and then they _____

4. They didn't _____ because they didn't have enough money.

5. They didn't _____. They listened to it.

Get Ready to Write

WRITING GOAL: Write a News Article

A news article has information about an event. It has a headline (title) and a byline (the writer's name). It answers the questions *who*, *what*, *where*, *when*, and *why*.

A Read the news article. Underline what the people said.

Writing Tip
Use quotation marks (" … ") to show what someone said.

Famous Rock Star at Rosemary School

by Samantha Johnson

The students at Rosemary School had a great party yesterday from 12 p.m. to 4:30 p.m. to end the school year. Everybody had food and drinks from the town's favorite restaurant, Joe's Pizza. And there was a special guest, too: the famous rock star Ricky Berry! He arrived at the party at 3:00 p.m. "This was once my school," he said, "so I'm really happy to be here!" He played his music, and everyone danced and took pictures.

B Look at **A**. What is the news article about? Complete the diagram.

Famous Rock Star at Rosemary School by Sam Johnson

Who?
1. _____Ricky Berry_____

What?
2. _____

Where?
3. _____

When?
4. _____

Why?
5. _____

Write

C Think about something that happened. Complete the diagram.

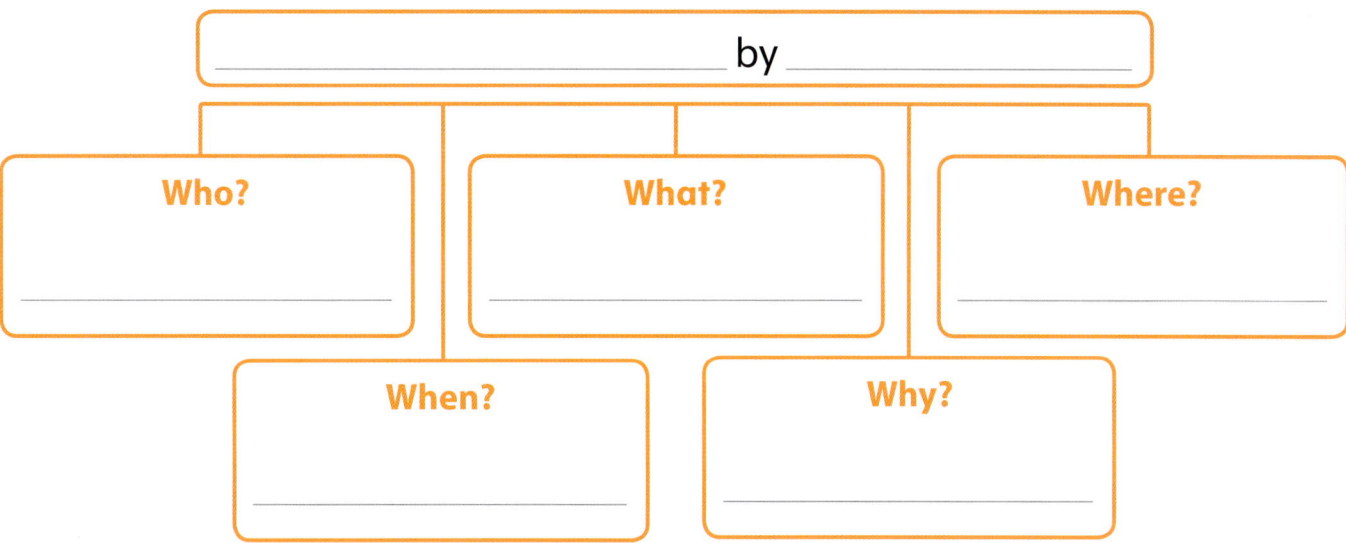

_____ by _____

Who?	What?	Where?
_____	_____	_____

When?	Why?
_____	_____

D Now write a news article. Use your ideas from **C**.
Then draw a picture of your story.

_____ by _____

_____

_____

_____

_____

_____

Now write another news article about something
else that happened.

MY WRITING GOAL

☐ I can write a news article.

Hop On, Hop Off!

MY GOALS

UNIT 11

- Read the story *Hurry!*
- Summarize

UNIT 12

- Read the blog *City Vacations*
- Identify facts and opinions

WRITE

- Write a story

A Look at the picture. What do you see?

1. What are the people doing?

2. Do you want to visit this place? Why or why not?

FUN FACT

Venice is a beautiful city in Italy, famous for its canals. There are pretty boats in these canals called *gondolas*. Venetians started using gondolas 950 years ago! The person who pushes a gondola is called a *gondolier*.

B Read the Fun Fact. Then answer the questions.

1. What is a gondola?
2. Do you like going on boat rides?

Think, Pair, Share
How is Venice different than where you live?

Get Ready to Read

READING GOAL: Summarize

Summarizing is telling what happened in a story in a few sentences. To summarize after you read, ask yourself, *What is the story about? What are the important events?*

A Look at the picture. What summarizes it best? Choose.

☐ a. a family vacation

☐ b. a school party

☐ c. a sports event

R Read and listen. 🔊 37

These are the important events of the story.

Owen's Trip to Venice

Owen's family does a lot on their trip to Venice, Italy. They go on a gondola ride around Venice. Owen takes a picture of the gondolier, Giancarlo, who's very funny. They also go to the famous St. Mark's Square. It's very crowded and Owen gets lost! Giancarlo helps Owen find his parents.

C Read **B** again. What is the best summary? Choose the correct answer.

☐ a. Owen takes a picture of Giancarlo.

☐ b. The family rides on a gondola.

☐ c. On a trip to Venice, Owen gets lost.

Read 38

What are the important events of the story? Underline them after you read.

– – Hurry! – –

On the way to the airport, May and her dad got stuck in traffic, and … oh no! Their car broke down. They ran out of gas, and they couldn't find a gas station. "We have to catch the subway, Dad!" May said.

"Quick!" shouted May's dad, as they ran through the closing doors. Just then … the lights went out. "Please get off the train. There's a problem with the track," said the conductor. "Come on! Hurry!" her dad said. They left the subway station quickly and got a taxi to the ferry. It took them under City Bridge and dropped them off at Ocean Station, where they caught a bus. The bus took them over Iron Bridge, and 15 minutes later, they arrived at the airport. "Hooray! We're on time. She doesn't have to wait," May's dad said.

"There she is!" shouted May, as she saw her mom walking toward them. "Welcome home!"

Think!

How do you get around your town or city?

Key Words 39

Listen, point, and say.

gas station

subway

through

ferry

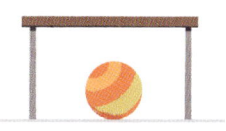

under

over

Find the key words in the story. Then write them in your picture dictionary.

Understand

Remember!
To **summarize** after you read, ask yourself, *What's the story about? What are the important events?*

A Read *Hurry!* again. Choose the best summary of the story.

☐ a. May and her dad got to the airport on time.

☐ b. May and her dad missed their flight.

B Choose the correct answer.

1. May and her dad are going to the **train station / airport**.

2. They ride **over / under** Iron Bridge on the bus.

3. They **are / aren't** on time to meet Mom at the airport.

C Complete the sentences.

| ferry | gas station | over | subway | through | under |

1.

They ran through closing doors onto the _____

2.

They need to find a _____ so they can refill their car.

3.

They go _____ City Bridge on the ferry.

4.

They ride _____ Iron Bridge on the bus.

D Look at the summary of *Hurry!* Complete the diagram.
Use *have to* and *doesn't have to*.

1. They ___have to___ get off the subway and get a taxi.

2. They _____ catch a ferry and then a bus to the airport.

A summary of Hurry!

3. They _____ go under City Bridge on the ferry.

4. May's mom _____ wait because they are on time.

E Look at **D**. Write. Use the correct form of *(not) have to* and the verb or verb phrase.

1.

May and her dad _____ _____ (get a taxi)

2.

They _____ _____ (catch a bus)

3.

They _____ _____ (ride a motorcycle)

4.

May's mom _____ _____ (wait)

MY READING GOALS

☐ I can read the story.

☐ I can identify the important events in a story and summarize them.

Get Ready to Read

READING GOAL: Identify Facts and Opinions
Writers can give their opinions and use facts to support them. When you read, decide what are facts and what are the writer's opinions.

A Look at the picture.
Underline the facts.
Circle the opinions.

1. There are tall buildings.

2. The statue is green.

3. The ferry is fun.

B Read and listen. 🔊 40

This is a **fact** and an (opinion).

I'm on Vacation!

I'm in New York City! It's the best city in the world. The buildings in Manhattan are so tall! I feel like an ant when I'm walking around the city. This morning we went on a boat tour and we visited the Statue of Liberty. It's amazing!

C Read **B** again. Are the statements Facts (F) or Opinions (O)? Choose F or O.

1. I'm in New York City! ☐ F ☐ O

2. We visited the Statue of Liberty. ☐ F ☐ O

3. It's amazing! ☐ F ☐ O

Read  41

Underline a **fact** and circle an **opinion** in each text.

www.cityvacations.osw/earth

City Vacations

Kim

Our next vacation is going to be in Bangkok, the biggest city in Thailand. It's famous for its beauty salons, but I think they're boring. I'm also going to go flowriding in Flow House Bangkok! It's like surfing, but the waves aren't real because it's inside. So cool!

Miranda

Our family is going to San Francisco! We're going to go on the cable cars and take pictures of the Golden Gate Bridge. It opened in 1937! We aren't going to go swimming in the ocean because it's too cold! I also want to go shopping. I think San Francisco has the best department stores in the US.

Mustafa

Dubai, here we come! I'm going to go to the top of a really tall skyscraper — the Burj Khalifa. It's 828 meters tall! We're also going to go to Mall of the Emirates, but we aren't going to go to the gift shops. We're going to go skiing inside the mall, instead! That's so cool!

Think!

What do you like to do when you're on vacation?

Listen, point, and say.

beauty salon

cable car

bridge

department store

skyscraper

gift shop

Find the key words in the texts. Then write them in your picture dictionary.

Understand

A Read *City Vacations* again. Are these opinions? Choose **Yes** or **No**.

1. Kim said flowriding is a sport you do inside.   **Yes**   **No**

2. Miranda thinks the Golden Gate Bridge is beautiful.   **Yes**   **No**

3. Mustafa thinks skiing inside the mall is cool.   **Yes**   **No**

B Choose the correct answer.

1. Kim's going to go flowriding in
   ☐ a. Flow House Bangkok.   ☐ b. Sea Life aquarium.

2. The Golden Gate Bridge opened in
   ☐ a. 2015.   ☐ b. 1937.

3. The Burj Khalifa is a
   ☐ a. mall.   ☐ b. skyscraper.

C Complete the sentences with key words. Then match.

1. Kim doesn't want to go to a _____

2. Miranda's going to go on a _____

3. Miranda's going to go shopping in a _____

4. Mustafa's going to go up a _____

a.    b.    c.    d.

_____   _____   _____   _____

D Work with a partner. Complete the diagram.

City Vacations

Miranda and family

Mustafa and family

1. We __are__ __going__ __to__ go on the cable cars.

2. We _____ _____ _____ swim in the ocean.

3. We _____ _____ _____ go to the mall.

4. We _____ _____ _____ go to the gift shops.

E Look at **D**. Write. Use *are going to* and *aren't going to*.

1.

They _____

_____ (gift shops)

2.

They _____

_____ (go skiing)

3.

They _____

_____ (ride cable cars)

4.

They _____

_____ (go swimming)

MY READING GOALS

☐ I can read the text.

☐ I can identify facts and opinions.

Reading Check

Remember!
To **summarize** a story or text, identify the important events. As you read, think about the writer's **opinions** and look for **facts** that support them.

A Read and listen. 🔊 43

To: Dad

From: Jack

Subject: I 💙 Sydney

Hi, Dad,

Sydney's amazing! Yesterday, we went on a ferry tour around Sydney Harbour. It took us under Sydney Harbour Bridge. We also walked over the bridge and I saw some tourists climbing it. It looked so scary! Oh, and I took pictures of the Sydney Opera House, one of the most beautiful buildings I've seen. I think it looks like sea shells.

We're in a department store now. Mom is looking around, and I'm having a sandwich and checking my e-mail. This afternoon, we have tickets to go up Sydney Tower, which is a skyscraper over 300 meters tall. Close to the top, at 250 meters, you can go outside and walk around the tower! It's called the Sydney Tower Eye, and our tickets include that, too. Anyway, I should go because we have to hurry and get the subway to the tower. We're having a lot of fun!

Lots of love,

Jack

B Look at Jack's e-mail. What's the best summary? Choose ✔ or ✘.

1. They have to take a subway to the tower.   ✔   ✘

2. They're having a lot of fun.   ✔   ✘

3. Jack is checking his e-mail.   ✔   ✘

C Look at what Jack wrote in his e-mail. Choose Fact (F) or Opinion (O).

1. I took pictures of the opera house.   F   O
2. I think it looks like sea shells.   F   O
3. I'm having a sandwich.   F   O

D Choose the correct answer.

1. What did Jack think was scary?
   ☐ a. climbing on the bridge   ☐ b. going on the ferry
2. What's Jack's mom doing now?
   ☐ a. shopping   ☐ b. having a snack
3. How tall is Sydney Tower?
   ☐ a. 250 meters   ☐ b. 300 meters
4. What are they going to do on the Sydney Tower Eye?
   ☐ a. climb to the top   ☐ b. walk around it
5. How are they going to get to Sydney Tower?
   ☐ a. on the subway   ☐ b. by bus

E Unscramble and match.

1. a s b w y u   •   • a. it joins two pieces of land
   _____

2. r y r f e   •   • b. a kind of boat
   _____

3. s y k s a p c e r r   •   • c. a very tall building
   _____

4. f g t i s o p h   •   • d. a kind of train
   _____

5. i b r e d g   •   • e. a store where you can buy
   _____   presents

Get Ready to Write

WRITING GOAL: Write a Story

A story has a setting, interesting characters, and a plot (beginning, middle, and end). It also has a problem and a solution.

A Read the story. Underline the speech tags.

> **Writing Tip**
> Use speech tags in your story. Speech tags tell you who is speaking and sometimes how words are said. Examples are *She said, I asked,* and *he cried.*

Where's My Koala?

Ellie loved her first visit to the zoo. At the end of the trip, she walked through the gift shop. "May I have that koala?" she asked as she pointed to a toy animal. "Yes! You've been good. You can have it," her dad said. After they left the shop, they took the subway to go shopping in a department store that's in a skyscraper. But when they got there, they had to run back to the subway. "Oh, no!" Ellie cried. "I dropped my koala on the platform!" "That's OK. We'll go back and find it," her dad said.

B Look at **A**. What is the problem and what is the solution? Complete the diagram.

Setting

1. the zoo, the subway

Characters

2. _____

Where's My Koala?

Problem

3. Ellie _____ on the platform.

Solution

4. They _____ to the subway.

Write

C Think of a new story with a problem and a solution. Complete the diagram.

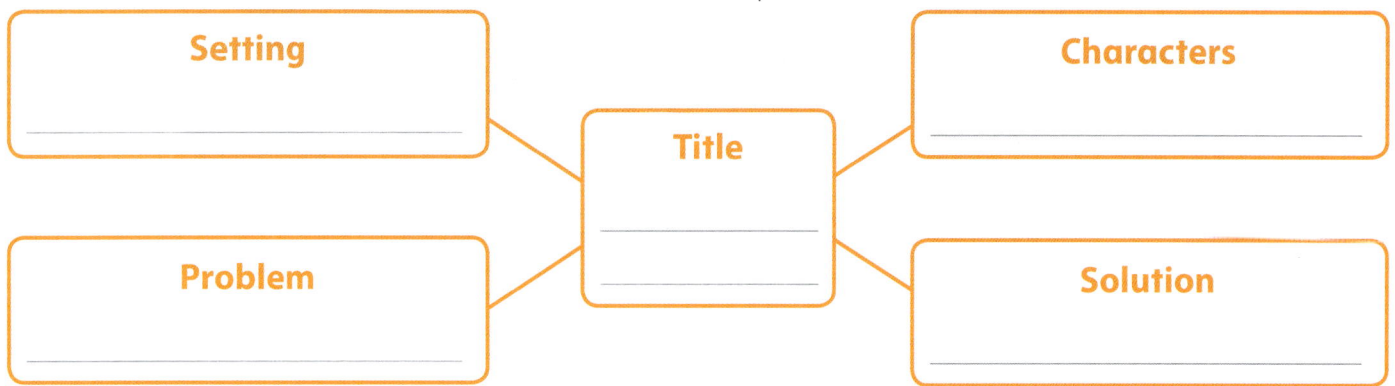

Setting	Title	Characters
_____	_____	_____

Problem		Solution
_____		_____

D Now write your story. Use your ideas from **C** and include dialogues. Then draw a scene from your story.

Title _____

_____

_____

_____

_____

_____

_____

Now write a similar story with a different problem and solution.

MY WRITING GOAL

☐ I can write a story and include dialogue.

Oxford Skills World

Reading with Writing 4

Workbook

Katie Foufouti

OXFORD
UNIVERSITY PRESS

Read

READING GOAL:
Identify Fiction and Nonfiction

Remember!
Fiction isn't true, and it has characters and colorful illustrations. **Nonfiction** gives information and it has facts, photos, and captions.

A Read the text. Notice if it is fiction or nonfiction. Circle the clues.

A New Goalie

"Come on! Get ready, girls!" Mr. Gomez, the soccer coach, shouted during practice. Vicky, the new player, started running with the other girls. She doesn't like sports much. She's good at badminton and ice hockey, but she's not very good at soccer. She has never scored a goal and she can't run very fast. "No one wants me on the team," she thought.

Score: 0–0

The next day, before the game, Vicky was a little nervous. Mr. Gomez told her she was going to be the goalie. She had never been a goalie before.

Both teams played well, but nobody won. Vicky stopped four goals! The score was 0–0. "You're the best goalie ever!" all the girls told her after the game. "Thanks!" she said. "I really like being a goalie!"

B Read the text again. Then choose the correct answer.

1. What can't you see in the story?
   - ☑ a. an illustration   ☐ b. a caption   ☐ c. a photo

2. What sport is the story about?
   - ☐ a. softball   ☐ b. badminton   ☐ c. soccer

3. After practice, Vicky felt
   - ☐ a. tired.   ☐ b. unhappy.   ☐ c. afraid.

4. During the game, Vicky discovered she
   - ☐ a. was a good goalie.   ☐ b. could score.   ☐ c. hated soccer.

C Trace the words. Then choose the correct picture for each word.

1. <u>play soccer</u>

☑ a.   ☐ b.

2. <u>play badminton</u>

☐ a.   ☐ b.

3. <u>team</u>

☐ a.   ☐ b.

4. <u>player</u>

☐ a.   ☐ b.

D Complete the sentences.

ball	coach	play ice hockey	~~play soccer~~	play badminton
	player	scores a goal	team	

1. You _____play soccer_____ with a big round ball. You have to run fast and kick the ball with your feet.

2. What's your favorite soccer _____? I like All Aces!

3. My friend Jack is the best soccer _____

4. He runs fast and always _____

5. I like to _____. It's like tennis , but I think it's a little easier to play.

6. I don't _____ because I can't skate.

Read

READING GOAL:
Identify the Writer's Purpose

A Read *School News*. Identify which paragraph gives information and which tries to persuade the reader to do something.

School News

Hello everyone!

We have some great news this week. Our basketball team is going to play in the final! They're playing against Mayflower Elementary School on Saturday. The game is at 10 a.m. at our sports center, if you want to come and watch.

Now, Mr. Barns, our softball coach, is still waiting for new players to join the softball team. Please talk to Mr. Barns and go to one of the softball practices. Don't worry if you don't know the rules. Mr. Barns likes to explain them, and he will help you understand them quickly. He'll show you how to catch the ball with the mitt and hit it with the bat.

That's all for today. Good luck to our basketball team and to Mr. Barns!

Mrs. Jones, Principal

B Read the announcement again. Then choose the correct answer.

The writer …

1. tells about a softball game.	**Yes**	(**No**)
2. tries to persuade the reader to join a team.	**Yes**	**No**
3. explains where and when the basketball game is.	**Yes**	**No**
4. says the softball team needs a new coach.	**Yes**	**No**
5. asks new players to talk to Mr. Barns.	**Yes**	**No**
6. explains the softball rules.	**Yes**	**No**

C Complete the sentences.

| mitt | catch the ball | bat | basketball | play softball | practice yoga |

1.

Let's _____

2.

I can't find my _____

3.

I like to _____

4.

Is he going to _____

D Complete the sentences.

You need this big glove to (1) _play_____ _softball_____.
It's called a (2) _m_____. You use it to (3) _c_____
_t_____ _b_____. You hit the ball with this stick. It's called a
(4) _b_____. So, who would like to join our team?

> **Remember!**
> Use words like *should*,
> *shouldn't*, *will*, and *won't* to
> persuade your readers.

Write

Underline the words that the writer uses to persuade.

Dear Uncle Jake,
You really shouldn't miss the tennis final tomorrow. It will be amazing
because two Spanish players are playing! Let's watch it together.
Bye,
Eddie

Read

READING GOAL:
Find the Main Idea
and Details

Remember!
A paragraph has a **main idea** and **details**. The details help you understand the main idea better.

A Read the article. Underline the main idea in each paragraph.

Forests in Danger

Our forests are in danger. About 30 percent of planet Earth is forest, but that number is going down. Scientists say that every year we lose about 70,000 square kilometers of forest. That's 3.5 to 7 billion trees!

There are many reasons for this, but some problems are worse than others. The biggest problem is that we cut down millions of trees every year to build houses and furniture, and to make paper. Another big problem is that it's getting hotter. Temperatures are rising and there is less rain and more forest fires.

So, what can we do to help? Buying things that are made with recycled paper and wood is better than buying new things. And try not to use too much water. Changing small things can make a big difference!

B Read the article again. Then choose the correct answer.

1. The main idea in the first paragraph is that forests are
   ☐ a. beautiful.   ☐ b. everywhere.   ☐ c. disappearing.

2. A detail about the main idea in the first paragraph is
   ☐ a. the danger.   ☐ b. 30 percent.   ☐ c. 70,000 square kilometers.

3. The second paragraph is about important
   ☐ a. problems.   ☐ b. forests.   ☐ c. people.

4. The third paragraph explains what we can do to protect
   ☐ a. paper.   ☐ b. forests.   ☐ c. water.

C Trace the words. Then choose the correct picture for each word.

1. Earth

☐ a.   ☐ b.

2. the sun

☐ a.   ☐ b.

3. sky

☐ a.   ☐ b.

4. cool

☐ a.   ☐ b.

D Complete the sentences.

| cool | Earth | sky | forest | warm | weather | lake | the sun |

1. You should wear a hat, sunglasses, and sunscreen to protect yourself from _____

2. It's getting really cold outside now. I can lend you this _____ sweater if you'd like.

3. Let's go swimming in the big _____

4. This forest is the most beautiful place on _____

5. Look at that cloud in the _____. It looks like a tree.

6. The _____ today is going to be warm and sunny.

Read

READING GOAL:
Make Predictions

> **Remember!**
> As you read the story, find clues to **predict** what will happen and how it will end.

A Look at the story. Predict what is going to happen. How is it going to end?

You Don't Need an Ax

Agu lived in a small village in the rain forest with his family. He grew up playing with forest animals and eating delicious tropical fruit.

One foggy day, Mother said, "We have no wood. I need some to cook." "I'll go get some," Grandfather said. Agu ran after him with his little ax.

They walked slowly through the rain forest. "Let's cut down this big tree, Grandpa!" Agu shouted. "No," Grandfather replied. "What about this one? Or that one?" Agu asked. Every time, Grandfather's answer was "No." Agu was disappointed. "We need the trees, Agu. They give us air to breathe and keep us dry in rainy weather," Grandfather explained. Agu understood now. "If we cut them down, soon there won't be any left," he said. "That's right," Grandfather said. "Here's some wood on the ground. Let's use this."

B Read the story again. Then choose the correct answer.

1. I made a correct prediction about the story.   **Yes**   **No**
2. Agu doesn't like to play with animals.   **Yes**   **No**
3. Agu's mother asked him to get some wood.   **Yes**   **No**
4. Agu wanted to cut down trees with his ax.   **Yes**   **No**
5. Agu's grandfather likes to cut down trees.   **Yes**   **No**
6. Agu learns that he should keep trees safe.   **Yes**   **No**

C Complete the sentences.

> foggy   humid   lake   rainbow   rain forest   tropical

1.

A beautiful _____ appeared behind the clouds.

2.

It's so _____ today. My hair and clothes feel wet.

3.

Pineapples and mangoes are my favorite _____ fruits.

4.

Tigers and monkeys live in the _____.

D Complete the sentences.

1. I'm visiting a r_____ f_____. There are lots of animals!

2. There's a l_____ and it's h_____. It's hard to stay dry.

3. After it rained, there was a beautiful r_____ in the sky.

Remember!
Use lots of adjectives to describe a place. Describe what you can see and hear.

Write

Underline the adjectives. What do they describe?

I live in a pretty town that's near a huge lake. In spring, there are lots of amazing birds at the lake and they're usually very noisy.

Read

READING GOAL:
Find Similes

A Find three similes. Underline them.

The Boy with Big Dreams

"Three … two … one … and liftoff!" There was fire and smoke under the rocket when it lifted off. Yuri held tightly to his seat inside the spacecraft. His heart was speeding like a race car. "In eight minutes," he thought, "I'll be in space!"

Then, suddenly, everything was as quiet as snow falling on the ground. Yuri looked out of the window. He saw Earth, and the moon was so close he thought he could see each and every little rock on it. When Yuri was a boy, people laughed when he said, "I want to go to space someday." "That's not possible," they said. Most boys his age wanted to sail a boat or climb mountains. But not Yuri. His dreams were big — as big as the Milky Way.

B Read the story again. Then choose the correct answer.

1. Yuri's heart was like a race car because it was going
   ☐ a. fast.   ☐ b. slowly.   ☐ c. loudly.

2. In space there was no
   ☐ a. light.   ☐ b. noise.   ☐ c. snow.

3. What did Yuri see from the window?
   ☐ a. our planet   ☐ b. the sun   ☐ c. the sky

4. People thought Yuri's dreams were
   ☐ a. possible.   ☐ b. interesting.   ☐ c. impossible.

C Trace the words. Then choose the correct picture for each word.

1. rocket

☐ a.   ☐ b.

2. rocks

☐ a.   ☐ b.

3. drive a race car

☐ a.   ☐ b.

4. sail a boat

☐ a.   ☐ b.

D Complete the sentences. Use the correct forms of the words.

volcano	drive a race car	rock	rocket
sail a boat	spacecraft	galaxy	Earth

1. Sam found a beautiful shell on a _____ at the beach.

2. They want to _____, but there's no wind.

3. You have to be careful around a _____. It can be dangerous!

4. The _____ flew straight up into the sky!

5. The astronauts sleep inside the _____

6. It's important to be safe. You must wear a helmet and a seatbelt to

_____

Read

READING GOAL:
Guessing Unknown Words

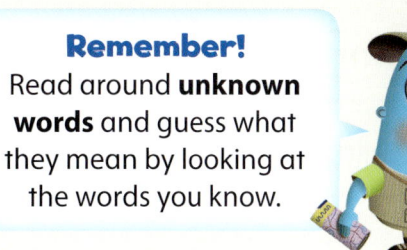
A Read the article. What do the underlined words mean?

Space Vacations

In the near future, maybe 50 or 100 years from now, astronauts won't be the only people to go to space. There will be special spacecraft, with passengers like you and me, traveling around our galaxy and the whole <u>universe</u>. We will build houses and cities on new planets.

Tickets for these kinds of trips will be expensive, of course. And the <u>flight</u> will be very long. Passengers will probably watch lots of movies and read many novels while they are traveling. Passengers should also be ready to <u>float</u> around the spacecraft. In space,

there's no gravity. That means that people and things have no weight to pull them down. It's almost like flying.

It's going to be exciting! Lots of people already want to buy tickets. Will you join them?

B Read the article again. Then choose the correct answer.

1. All the stars, planets, and galaxies are the *universe*.   **Yes**   **No**
2. People will read more novels in space.   **Yes**   **No**
3. It'll be cheap to travel to space.   **Yes**   **No**
4. In the future, more people will travel to space.   **Yes**   **No**
5. To float, you sit on the ground.   **Yes**   **No**
6. People today aren't interested in traveling to space.   **Yes**   **No**

C Complete the sentences.

| build a house | suitcase | city | passengers | read a novel | travel around |

1.

I don't live in a _____.
I live in a village.

2.

Your _____
is too heavy to lift!

3.

When I'm traveling, I always
_____

4.

_____ on
planes must wear seatbelts.

D Complete the sentences.

I'm (1) r_____ a n_____ about a man who wanted to
(2) b_____ a h_____ on the moon. When he got there, he saw
a big (3) c_____ with people, so he unpacked his (4) s_____ and
looked around.

Write

Remember!
Use transitions to organize an opinion text.

Underline the transition words.

Space is an amazing place. First, we don't know where it ends.
Next, it's full of beautiful stars and planets.

Read

READING GOAL:
Compare and Contrast

Remember!
Both, *too*, and *similar* show similarities. *But*, *different*, and *unlike* show differences.

A Read *Dolly and Polly*. Underline a similarity and a difference in the text.

Dolly and Polly

My favorite toys are these two dolls, Dolly and Polly. I saw them in the store and my mom bought them for me. I was so happy! I always keep them on my bed, and I can't sleep without them.

Dolly and Polly look alike. I think they're sisters. They both have bangs and ponytails. Dolly's hair is purple and curly. Polly's hair is curly, too, but it's green. Unlike Dolly, Polly has freckles on her nose and cheeks. They're wearing similar dresses and shoes. Dolly's dress is pink with white flowers. Polly's dress is blue with small, yellow stars. I need to wash their dresses because they're both a little dirty. My little sister likes to play with them and her hands aren't always very clean.

B Read the story again. Then choose the correct answer.

1. What does only one doll have?
   ☐ a. bangs   ☐ b. a ponytail   ☐ c. freckles

2. Both dolls have
   ☐ a. curly hair.   ☐ b. green hair.   ☐ c. shoulder-length hair.

3. The dolls' dresses are both
   ☐ a. white.   ☐ b. dirty.   ☐ c. short.

4. Which dress has yellow stars?
   ☐ a. Dolly's   ☐ b. Polly's   ☐ c. both dresses

C Trace the words. Then choose the correct picture for each word.

1. _____bangs_____

☐ a.   ☐ b.

2. _____curly_____

☐ a.   ☐ b.

3. _____freckles_____

☐ a.   ☐ b.

4. _____blond_____

☐ a.   ☐ b.

D Complete the sentences.

| bangs curly freckles shoulder-length |
| short a ponytail blond straight |

1. Polly has green, _____ hair.

2. Dolly doesn't have _____ on her nose and cheeks.

3. They both have _____ and wear their hair in _____

4. Their hair isn't _____. It's longer.

5. Dolly's hair isn't _____. It's purple.

Read

READING GOAL:
Understanding Characters

Remember!
Look at what the
character says and does
to help you **understand**
how he or she feels.

A Read the story. Underline what Carla says and does that shows her feelings.

A Present for Ed

Carla searched the gift shop, but couldn't find the action figure Ed wanted. She asked a clerk for help. "It's for my nephew. It's his birthday today," she explained. The clerk didn't know this toy. "What does it look like?" he asked. Carla looked at the photo Ed texted her and explained, "It's tall and has curly, dark hair. It doesn't have a beard or moustache. It's wearing a blue suit and a pink cape."

The clerk looked around the store, too, but he couldn't find the toy. "Oh no! The party's in 15 minutes," Carla said. "What am I going to do?" But what was that, there, hiding behind that box? "It's the last Strongman!" the clerk said. "Hooray! Thank you!" Carla said. She paid and ran off to Ed's party.

B Read *A Present for Ed* again. Then choose the correct answer.

1. "Oh no!" means that Carla is worried.   **Yes**   **No**

2. "Hooray!" means Carla is happy.   **Yes**   **No**

3. Strongman has curly orange hair.   **Yes**   **No**

4. Strongman doesn't have a beard.   **Yes**   **No**

5. The clerk knows what Strongman looks like.   **Yes**   **No**

6. The store was closed when Carla got there.   **Yes**   **No**

C Complete the sentences.

a beard	glasses	a moustache	old	curly	tall

1.

Ed isn't _____.

He's a little boy.

2.

Strongman's hair is short and

_____

3.

Strongman doesn't have

_____

4.

Strongman isn't short. He's

_____

D Complete the sentences.

1. My sister has short, s_____ hair and f_____

2. My eyes are strong, so I don't need to wear g_____

3. Eric wants to be a t_____ basketball player.

Write

Underline phrases that describe what Mr. Oliver looks like.

Mr. Oliver is my English teacher. He's not short or very tall. He has curly, brown hair and blue eyes. He always wears glasses and really colorful T-shirts. I really like him!

Read

READING GOAL:
Cause and Effect

A Read the text. Underline the causes and circle the effects.

Joey Wins *Kids with Talent* by Lisa May

This year the winner of *Kids with Talent* is Joey Wilson. There were a lot of children who played music on the TV show, but not like Joey played the piano. "If you keep practicing, you'll be the best piano player in the country one day," rock star Eddie Parker said.

After four weeks on the show, Joey is back home. He slept late today because he was up late with his family. "We had a big party! Everyone wanted to take a picture with me at my piano, so I felt like a famous rock star," Joey laughed. He looked again at the big, black piano and smiled. "I can't believe it's mine," he said. "I'm going to play every day, so I can go to music college someday," he explained.

B Read the text again. Then choose the correct answer.

1. Joey will become a great piano player if he
   ☐ a. plays with Eddie. ☐ b. wins the show. ☐ c. practices.

2. Joey was on *Kids with Talent* for
   ☐ a. two weeks. ☐ b. three weeks. ☐ c. four weeks.

3. Joey slept late because he had a party with
   ☐ a. classmates. ☐ b. his family. ☐ c. rock stars.

4. Joey felt famous because everyone wanted to
   ☐ a. take a photo with him. ☐ b. hear him play.
   ☐ c. see his new piano.

C Trace the words. Then choose the correct picture for each word.

1. _____ sleep late _____   2. _____ have a party _____

☐ a.   ☐ b.   ☐ a.   ☐ b.

3. _____ take a picture _____   4. _____ send a text _____

☐ a.   ☐ b.   ☐ a.   ☐ b.

D Complete the sentences.

| had a party | met a rock star | played music | sent a text |
| slept late | took pictures | won a prize | sang a song |

1. Joey _____ on the TV show called *Kids with Talent*.
   It was Eddie Parker!

2. Joey didn't sing on the TV show. He _____

3. Joey _____ to his friends with his phone.

4. After the show, Joey _____ at his house.

5. Joey's family _____ with him. All the attention
   made him feel like a rock star!

6. The next day, Joey _____. He was tired from the
   party the night before.

Read

READING GOAL:
Find the Theme

Remember!
Every story has a **theme** or a lesson you can learn. To find it, think about what the characters do.

A Read the story. Underline the theme.

We Found This!

The lights went on in the movie theater. "I really liked it," Mark said to his sister. "Me too," Jenny said. Then she saw a cell phone on the floor. She picked it up and the screen went on. "Hey! Cool pictures," Mark said. There was a man with a beard and glasses in the pictures. "Look! He went bowling and he flew a kite at the beach!" Mark said. "Oh no!" The screen went off. "We shouldn't play with other people's things," Jenny said, and they took it to the ticket seller. "Excuse me. We found this," Mark explained. "Whose is it?" the woman asked. "It's mine. Thank you so much!" said a man with a beard and glasses. He turned the phone on and walked away. "I'm glad we didn't break it!" said Mark.

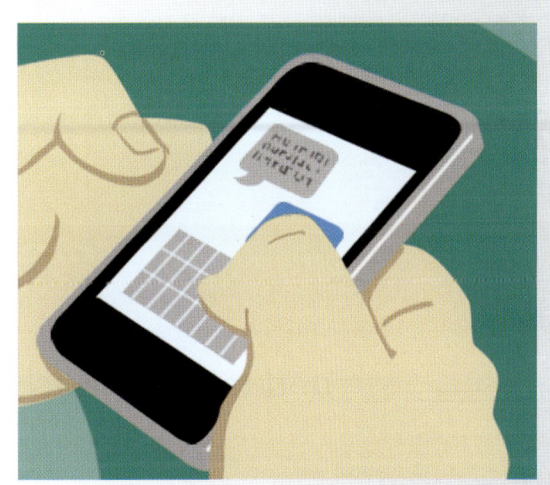

B Read the story. Then choose the correct answer.

1. The theme is *Don't play with other people's things.*   **Yes**   **No**

2. Mark and Jenny didn't enjoy the movie.   **Yes**   **No**

3. Mark didn't like the pictures on the cell phone.   **Yes**   **No**

4. The man flew a kite at the beach.   **Yes**   **No**

5. Mark and Jenny should've kept the phone.   **Yes**   **No**

6. The man had a beard and glasses.   **Yes**   **No**

C **Complete the sentences.**

found money	flew a kite	went bowling
went to the mall	saw a movie	advertisement

1.

Last weekend I _____
_____ with my friends.

2.

We _____
_____ and had lunch.

3.

Kay _____
_____ and told our teacher.

4.

We saw an _____
for ice cream.

D **Complete the sentences.**

1. On Saturday, I w_____ to the m_____ with my friends.

2. Should we f_____ a k_____ or g_____ b_____

Write

What do the people say? Underline.

Ben, the man with the beard and glasses, wanted to thank Mark and Jenny because they found his phone. "I'm going to buy you tickets for the movie next Sunday," he said. "Wow! Thanks!" Jenny and Mark said.

Remember!
Use quotation marks ("…") to show what someone said.

Read

READING GOAL:
Summarize

Remember!
To **summarize** a story, explain what happens in a few sentences.

A Read the story. Underline the important events.

Nowhere like Venice

Piero is a gondolier in Venice. Every day, he takes people through the canals in his gondola. He loves singing as his gondola slides on the water under the bridges. The tourists stop to wave at Piero and take pictures of him. "I'm going to be a famous singer," Piero says.

One day, Piero says goodbye to his friends and family, and takes a ferry. He goes to a big city where he sings in theaters and restaurants. For a year, he has to take the subway and walk through crowded streets. He has no friends and he misses Venice. One morning, Piero wakes up and says to himself, "I don't have to stay. I'm going back!" Piero is happy and everyone can hear his beautiful voice around Venice again.

B Read the story again. Then choose the correct answer for each question.

1. What is a good sentence to summarize the story?
   ☐ a. Piero is only happy in Venice.
   ☐ b. Piero has a good time in the city.
   ☐ c. Piero works as a gondolier.

2. What do the tourists do when they hear Piero sing?
   ☐ a. sing with him   ☐ b. laugh at him   ☐ c. photograph him

3. How does Piero move around the city?
   ☐ a. by ferry   ☐ b. by bus   ☐ c. on the subway

4. Piero decides to leave the city because he's
   ☐ a. unhappy.   ☐ b. famous.   ☐ c. bored.

C Trace the words. Then choose the correct picture for each word.

1. _____ferry_____

☐ a.   ☐ b.

2. _____over_____

☐ a.   ☐ b.

3. _____subway_____

☐ a.   ☐ b.

4. _____through_____

☐ a.   ☐ b.

D Complete the sentences.

ferry	gas station	over	subway	through
	under	gondola	bicycle	

1. Ali turned on the lights as he drove _____ the tunnel.

2. Can you stop at the _____? We need to fill up the car with gas.

3. We took the _____ to get to the island and we saw dolphins!

4. Don't jump _____ the gate. It's dangerous.

5. I found your sock. It was _____ the bed.

6. We took the _____ to go downtown.

Read

READING GOAL:
Identifying Facts and Opinions

Remember!
As you read, notice the writer's **opinions** and the **facts** he or she uses to support them.

A Read the text. What's the writer's opinion of the city?

Istanbul by Elif

Istanbul is a very big city by the sea. One part of it is in Europe and the other in Asia. The sea is in the middle, and the Bosphorus Bridge joins both parts. At night, the bridge lights up and the sea is full of little lights, too.

One of my favorite things to do in Istanbul is take a ferry and visit the small island of Buyukada. I also like to walk around the Grand Bazaar. It was built in 1461! You can find really nice gifts there. You don't need to go to a gift shop or a big department store. There aren't many skyscrapers in this city, but there are lots of beautiful old buildings. I think Istanbul is a great place! I'm going to visit it again next year!

B Read the text. Then choose the correct answer.

1. In Elif's opinion, Istanbul is a great city.   **Yes**   **No**
2. Istanbul is by the sea and this is a fact.   **Yes**   **No**
3. Elif says the Bosphorus Bridge is ugly.   **Yes**   **No**
4. Elif often goes on short trips around Istanbul.   **Yes**   **No**
5. Elif prefers shopping in department stores.   **Yes**   **No**
6. Elif is planning to visit Istanbul soon.   **Yes**   **No**

C Complete the sentences.

beauty salon	bridge	cable car
department store	gift shop	skyscraper

1.

My favorite _____ is the Flatiron Building.

2.

The _____ is almost 3 kilometers long.

3.

My aunt works in a

_____

4.

The Science Museum has a really cool _____

D Complete the sentences.

Take the (1) s_____ to the (2) b_____ s_____ for a hair cut. After, you can walk over the (3) b_____ to the (4) d_____ s_____. It's right next to a giant (5) s_____.

Write

Remember!
Use speech tags to show who is speaking and how words are said.

Underline the speech tags.

"Welcome home!" Piero's friends and family shouted as he walked into the surprise party. "Are you glad to be back home?" his mom asked. "Yes. I'm the happiest person in Venice!" said Piero. "That's good, because we won't ever let you leave again," they said. Everyone laughed.

Picture Dictionary

Unit 1

_____

_____

_____

_____

_____

_____

Unit 2

_____

_____

_____

_____

_____

_____

Unit 3

_____

_____

_____

_____

_____

_____

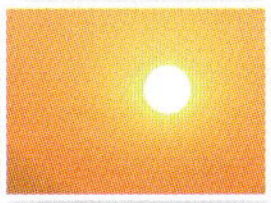

Unit 4

_____

_____

_____

_____

_____

_____

Picture Dictionary

Unit 5

_____

_____

_____

_____

_____

_____

Unit 6

_____

_____

_____

_____

_____

_____

Unit 7

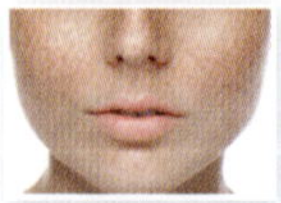

_____

_____

_____

_____

_____

_____

Unit 8

_____

_____

_____

_____

_____

Unit 9

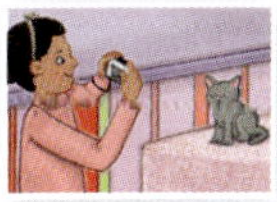

_____

_____

_____

_____

_____

_____

Unit 10

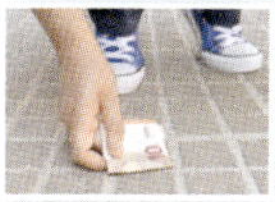

_____

_____

_____

_____

_____

_____

Unit 11

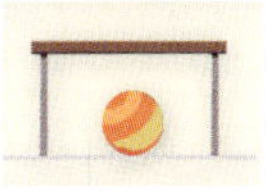

_____

_____

_____

_____

_____

_____

Unit 12

_____

_____

_____

_____

_____

_____

Syllabus

Topic	Unit	Reading Goal	Key Words	Writing Goal
TOPIC 1 Crazy About Sports!	Unit 1	Identify Fiction and Nonfiction	*team, player, score a goal, play soccer, play badminton, play ice hockey*	Write a Persuasive Text
	Unit 2	Identify the Writer's Purpose	*play softball, catch the ball, mitt, bat, basketball, practice yoga*	Focus: Persuasive words
TOPIC 2 The Living Earth	Unit 3	Find the Main Ideas and Details	*Earth, warm, the sun, sky, weather, cool*	Write a Descriptive Text
	Unit 4	Make Predictions	*tropical, rain forest, humid, lake, foggy, rainbow*	Focus: Adjectives
TOPIC 3 Let's Go to Space!	Unit 5	Find Similes	*spacecraft, rocks, rocket, sail a boat, volcano, drive a race car*	Write an Opinion Text
	Unit 6	Guess Unknown Words	*travel around, passenger, suitcase, read a novel, city, build a house*	Focus: Transition words and phrases
TOPIC 4 Looks and Feelings	Unit 7	Compare and Contrast	*curly, blond, a ponytail, shoulder-length hair, bangs, freckles*	Write a Descriptive Text
	Unit 8	Understand Characters	*old, tall, straight, a moustache, a beard, glasses*	Focus: Intensifiers
TOPIC 5 What Happened?	Unit 9	Understand Cause and Effect	*sleep late, have a party, meet a rock star, play music, send a text, take a picture*	Write a News Article
	Unit 10	Find the Theme	*find money, go to the mall, see a movie, go bowling, advertisement, fly a kite*	Focus: Quotation marks
TOPIC 6 Hop On, Hop Off!	Unit 11	Summarize	*gas station, subway, through, ferry, under, over*	Write a Story
	Unit 12	Identify Facts and Opinions	*beauty salon, cable car, bridge, department store, skyscraper, gift shop*	Focus: Speech tags